CITY
MANAGEMENT
SNAPSHOTS

On The Run

BY

BEN LEITER

Acknowledgements

The author wishes to acknowledge the cartoons contributed by Douglas Harman. The author has been an enthusiastic fan of Doug's artwork for over thirty years.

Over the decades, Doug has brought color to our bureaucratic gray and a smile to our faces. We found ourselves in need of both.

While Mr. Harman is an accomplished City Manager in his own right, hence the poignancy of his cartoons, these are not his stories; but, he would probably tell you, they could be.

The author would also like to thank his lovely wife and their three wonderful children who put up with him and these adventures over the decades. It wasn't easy for them. But, they are now of an age when they can appreciate what it was all about.

About The Author

Ben Leiter "enjoyed" a forty-four-year career in public management. During that time he served in five states across the country, in a total of eleven jurisdictions, with a collection of seventeen job titles, seven of which were "City Manager."

Other titles included: Assistant City Manager, Deputy City Manager, Budget Director, Redevelopment and Economic Development Director, and Housing Field Representative for the Human Relations Commission.

Ben formally represented the International City Management Association (ICMA) and the United States three times in overseas delegations. He could not just go along for the ride and had to turn two of them into major adventures.

Mr. Leiter earned two master's degrees along the way.

He has spoken at the annual ICMA conference, at state city management associations, and also at the Government Finance Officers Association of Texas. Finance directors do have a sense of humor.

Mr. Leiter has published articles in professional publications; written newspaper columns; and appeared on local government television shows.

Ben Leiter has been subjected to reporting in daily newspapers ranging from *The Washington Post* to *The Dallas Morning News* to *The Los Angeles Times*.

Besides retaining anonymity, another reason for the pseudonym is to keep the motivation pure in the tale telling.

William Kirchhoff, the City Manager of five cities and an adjunct professor at five schools of public administration says:

"By any standards, the author is one of the country's most accomplished City Managers. Few in the profession have his experience; fewer yet match his level of accomplishment. His honesty, character, and respect for the public have well served the communities he has managed. His stories, some defying belief, are true. Many of us have been there."

Mr. Kirchhoff has written numerous professional books and a suspense novel, *Heavy Air*.

TABLE OF CONTENTS

INTRODUCTION

UNFORTUNATELY, IT'S ALL TRUE.
Or, at least it's my truth.

I present professional life snapshots of conflict, corruption, character assassination, betrayal, murder, suicide, drug running, spying, sex scandals, courage, heroes, and a monkey on the loose. Most days were meetings.

This is my story as a municipal bureaucrat, spanning forty-four years.

I am a gray man. My training and environment dictated planned, constrained, organizational nuance. Budgets, staff meetings, zoning hearings, union negotiations, and more meetings constituted my world.

I encountered the best and the worst in people. On one level, this is just a City Manager memoir; on another, it reflects themes in everyone's life journey.

What is that old saying? "We make plans, and God laughs." I made lots of plans. God looked at me, and She is in hysterics. Poor, poor gray man.

I present this story to you in candid, rapid-fire snapshots. No specific individual or city is identified. This protects the innocent and, unfortunately, the guilty, too. Camouflaged with anonymity and the pseudonym Ben Leiter, I can tell my story the way it needs to be told. Truth.

I have served all over the country.

As a young person struggling to make the right career choice, I wanted my work to make a meaningful contribution, and I didn't want to be bored.

I have not been bored.

After you read this book, if you should run into the City Manager of your community, just say "thanks." He or she will know what you mean.

WHY TELL ALL?

This is dedicated to the next generation of City Managers. You, too, may enjoy similar adventures! Please march forward with your ideals and optimism and desire to improve the way things are. But just know, from these snapshots, that the profession can sometimes be a swamp with different kinds of alligators. Be prepared.

You, who are about to embark, I salute you!

A former boss of mine, describing the job of city management, said, "When it's going well, it's the best job in the world. When it isn't, it's hell."

Anyone thinking about becoming a City Manager needs to know what really goes on behind the scenes, beyond the press releases, the ribbon cuttings, and the smiling handshakes to understand this challenging professional world.

I have concluded that to be a good City Manager, you will have to stand up, at some time, for the right thing. It doesn't matter how diplomatic you are, how expertly you process issues, how well you keep your bosses informed. At some point, there will be consequences.

A former colleague of mine, whom I regard as one of the icons of the city management profession, wrote a professional tract entitled "Conflict Management in the Public Arena: Lessons

Learned from the Art of War." The pressures of the profession require you to work for an elected board, keep them happy if you want to keep your job, and stand tall when required. Keep the writings of Sun Tzu in your briefcase.

As I thought about it more, I realized I felt like Private Ryan at the end of the Steven Spielberg movie. Ryan went through horrendous World War II combat in his youth. Many people sacrificed for him.

Ryan, fifty years later, returns to the European grave of his commanding officer. He turns to his wife and says, "Tell me I've led a good life. Tell me I'm a good man."

WHAT A CRAZY WAY
TO MAKE A LIVING!

Following the city attorney down the hall after a council meeting one night, I started to say something, then thought better of it. He might not understand. To my astonishment, the city attorney blurted out what I was thinking, word for word, "What a crazy way to make a living!"

After a full day of work, it was an evening meeting that had started at six, adjourned at ten thirty, and required our studied participation. We were just tired.

We chatted for a moment about the frustrations and the peak experiences. We wondered if we were "adrenaline junkies" needing the tension of the latest controversy.

The reasons for these narrative snapshots emerged because the stories of veteran City Managers always stuck with me. I remember them all, decades later. Professional case studies and academic course work educated me along the way—but I don't remember them well.

I recall the real people with blood, sweat, and tears, and the pain in their soft undertones and in their eyes. If you have chosen the city management profession and read this monograph, you will receive the benefit of years' worth of hallway conversations at the ICMA Conferences.

I have deliberately slid back and forth in time and place with the snapshots in order to make it almost impossible to identify specific places and people.

Selah.

WHAT IS A CITY MANAGER?

The City Manager is the business manager of the day-to-day affairs of the municipal government.

This form of government is known as the Council/Manager Plan. About half of all US municipalities have adopted this type of government. The genesis of this profession was the "good government reform movement" at the turn of the last century. That good government reformer ethos drives the self-imposed ethics and passion underlying many encounters in these snapshots.

The Council/Manager Plan is based on the corporate model of formal organization. In a corporation, a board of directors sets overall policy and direction. The day-to-day running of the corporation is performed by the chief executive officer.

In the Council/Manager Plan, the city council serves as the elected board of directors for the municipal corporation. The City Manager acts as the chief executive and may go by other titles, such as city administrator.

How and why did I become a City Manager? Some or all of the following may explain it.

My adult political consciousness was formed in the 1960s when it was fashionable to ask what you could do for your country or your community in the way of public service. It seemed to be a time when a person, or a few people, could make a real difference.

There was a history of public service in my family. My father had been the president of the Chamber of Commerce in our community, and my mother had been vice president of the League of Women Voters. My father always held our local City Manager in high esteem, saying he was the only one who made any sense and didn't play politics with every issue.

My father was a lifelong Republican; my mother was a lifelong Democrat. Today, I find myself a committed nonpartisan and figure it is my genetic inheritance.

My religious tradition proclaimed that one of the highest forms of human activity was service to community. It probably also contained a dose of the American theologically based work ethic of "salvation through good works."

In college, I had a wonderful opportunity for a summer internship in a City Manager's Office. The City Manager, then, was considered one of the best in the country and a model of suave, efficient management. I went into that experience expecting to be working with "gray men" — bureaucrats interested only in shuffling paper and totally lacking in personality. Instead, I found dedicated, hardworking civil servants who took their jobs seriously. They also accepted with relative grace and good humor the ever-present public scrutiny and second-guessing of their actions.

To this day, I still marvel that a finance director could have such a wonderful sense of humor.

The other side of that coin exposed lackluster folks too and a workplace commitment to status quo and routine. I believed with my crusading spirit and some talent I could stand out. It looked like fun.

I did the math. It's a big country with thousands of cities, counties and special jurisdictions. You take that number and multiply it by the positions of manager or administrator, deputy, and department head, and you are looking at over ten thousand jobs. I calculated significant career opportunity, where I could spread my wings. I concluded that as long as I was willing to pick up and move somewhere in this huge country and continent, I should be able to have a job. That turned out to be the case.

In high school, I took guidance tests designed to identify aptitude for various careers. I scored high as a social worker and as an accountant.

After forty four years in the city management business, much of my time has been spent using those two skills.

However, given the difficult interpersonal relationships among some of the elected boards I have worked with, more training in dysfunctional family dynamics would have been helpful.

WHAT IS COURAGE?

Finding *COURAGE* and having to use it along the career journey has been an uncomfortable experience. It has required soul-searching, anxiety, and self-doubt.

The situations requiring courage usually involved one or more of my elected officials "stepping out of bounds." That bad behavior ranged from inappropriately chastising my staff in public to suspected graft and corruption.

I have been required to confront one of my worst fears: getting fired. However, later in my career, with a strong résumé, that perspective changed in a viciously challenging political environment.

There, my worst fear centered on elected officials poised to destroy my reputation or to find some way to ruin me. I stood in the way of their nefarious schemes to abuse power and reap financial gain at public expense.

It was so bad I harbored fantasies of precipitating an immediate dismissal so that I could take a six-month vacation and find a less totally dysfunctional elected body.

Interestingly, it was much easier to confront black-and-white situations, no matter how difficult, where I had no choice but to do the right thing. However, when the situation was more a shade of gray, it required more self-examination.

Along the way, there were many shades of gray.

ADVENTURES ALONG THE WAY

The 60s and 70s

The warm summer evening drew to a pleasant close in 1967 as dusk fell. I was still on my mission-driven quest conducting an opinion survey for the city on open housing, in the exclusive all-white suburb in the Midwest, next to the medium-sized city that I worked for.

I approached the next house and informed the homeowner of my purpose. The middle-aged homeowner, instead of responding to my survey questions, paternally advised me in ironic tones that I ought to be careful. Since it was dark, I might be mistaken for a burglar and get shot!

I sensed a mixed message. As I continued walking down the street, the realization struck like a fired bullet. That was the first time in my career I had been threatened to be shot.

It had been a walk on the darkside.

It was the late 1960s in the Midwest, and American cities were burning. My boss's city job mandated improving race relations in the community. He was Black.

US Army intelligence had just informed him that Stokley Carmichael had slipped into the ghetto the night before. Stokley was meeting with neighborhood "radicals." I was fascinated with my insider vantage point, knowing the real story behind the daily news reporting.

I knew my boss well, but not intimately, because it was too risky for him to cross the racial divide with complete trust. In some quarters he was labeled an Uncle Tom; in others, he was seen as a mediator. I knew him to be a skilled, compassionate man, deeply committed to improved race relations between Whites and Blacks.

I also knew that he understood the different roles that had to be played in the American drama of race relations. My boss had his role to play. He was being paid to keep the lid on things.

Stokley had his role: BURN, BABY, BURN!

Although my boss publicly disavowed Stokley Carmichael's tactics, he knew the 1960s Black insurrection had propelled his own job into the importance of putting out racial fires.

It was just so hard to get White folks to wake up and pay attention! Stokley had a way of getting people's attention. It was a very expensive wake-up call for America.

Today was the election of the neighborhood council. My assignment, representing the City Manager's Office, required me to monitor the neighborhood voting to ensure a clean election. The neighborhood council exercised great influence over federal grants brought in to renew the community. The feds were experimenting with modern democracy at the neighborhood level; a tricky business.

At the elementary school, in the all-Black neighborhood, folks were standing in line to vote. The street grapevine whispered that the incumbent head of the neighborhood council was paying transients to vote in support of his candidates.

I went over to the polling place to see first hand. Right away, the six-foot-four-inch, 240-pound, muscle-endowed, very loud chairman confronted me. His three toughs-in-tow immediately flanked me. I held my ground with an impassive face, working to hide my nervous tension.

I asserted my right to observe polling procedures. The street-lingo responses were unflattering to my ancestral lineage and to my mother.

As long as I wasn't physically accosted, there was no need to call for help.

Suddenly, he grabbed my arm. I shook free and walked to the office and called the police. My boss showed up and defused the situation about thirty minutes later. The back and forth jawing consumed most of the morning. I later found out that it had all been a ruse to distract me while they ran the transient "voters" through to elect their candidates.

Not the best side of American democracy at work.

Check For Guns

In the medium-sized midwest city's meeting with the neighborhood council, personally representing the City Manager's office, I looked down at the open briefcase of the gentleman next to me. Staring up at me from the briefcase was a chrome-plated revolver. I knew I was in a tough neighborhood, and I knew this could be a tough business, but it wasn't that tough, was it?

I have remembered that incident over the years as I have run into difficult conversations with elected officials, union representatives, unhappy staff, and others. In those situations, I have reminded myself that while the conversation may be uncomfortable, at least we are not talking about guns in briefcases. (At least not that I knew of.)

In the large midwest city I served in, a heavily armed policeman in civilian clothes sat in the reception area all day long because of death threats against the mayor. Four months earlier, a crazed gunman had stormed through the office, threatening staff.

"Fire The Staff"

One day in the medium-sized western city, I received a visit from the new mayor. He wanted to chat. According to the mayor, we had staff who "weren't with the program." He said he knew I hadn't hired them; but, the longer they stayed, the more I would be identified with them.

Curious, I asked, "Who is the problem, Mayor?" He urged me to find a way to get rid of the police chief, the city clerk, the city attorney, the city planner, and the city engineer.

Ironically, these were the best performers in the organization. They did their jobs well and exhibited a professional sense of public service.

I was totally furious and calm at the same time. I had NEVER before been confronted with such a wrongful, outrageous suggestion from an elected official.

Considering the circumstances and my feelings at the moment, I gave one of the most diplomatic responses of my professional life. I asked him why he felt that way and then further responded by saying, "Uh-huh," and "I see." That was the end of that conversation. No heads rolled on my watch in that city.

Of course, he easily figured out that he could best remove the targeted staff by removing me, and so he started working on that human resources strategy.

I was impressed that, mentally, I had spent no time weighing what to do. There was no hesitation regarding his silly demands. The mayor's neighbor described him as, "Waking up in the morning, and it's a different world every day."

Initially, I didn't understand what that meant. However, continued inconsistent interactions on his part made it clear.

Maybe I had the right stuff after all?

Years later, a successor to my City Manager job in that same city resigned with a settlement in excess of seven hundred thousand dollars.

"FIRE THE CITY MANAGER"

I found this bit of information out, ten years after the fact.

The good ole boy mayor had gone into closed session with the council and said, "We need to get ourselves a new City Manager, one whose wife can speak English."

(My wife is Hispanic. English is her second language. She is also a sweet, gentle person.)

I couldn't believe this phone conversation with the former council member.

"Why didn't you tell me that when it happened?" I nearly yelled on the phone.

He replied, "How are you feeling right now?"

I responded, "I want to go kill the SOB."

He replied, "That's why I didn't tell you."

THE CITY MANAGER IS AWESOME!

My City Manager job in the large western city required that I sit up on the city council dais with the elected officials. The meeting had started at 8:40 AM. It was now 3:20 PM. The president of the largest of our eight employee unions had been hanging around the council chamber all afternoon. I assumed he was going to say something to the council, under the public comment portion of the agenda.

Not only were the meetings open to the public, but they were broadcast live and replayed during the week. Great show…for insomniacs.

Over the years, I had dealt with many union officers. This one wasn't bad, just sort of mouthy, complaining about one thing or another, and certainly never had a good word for anyone in management. In his eyes it always seemed like we suits just didn't get it.

The union president stood up, approached the speaker's podium. "You all know me. I'm here today to talk about your City Manager."

My heart sank and then started its Indianapolis Speedway racing, which usually occurred when I was being attacked publicly. My eyes narrowed, another defensive idiosyncrasy. I also wanted a bathroom break but that wasn't going to happen.

"He's awesome!" he blurted out. "He has kept his word to us on everything he promised. He introduced this high performance training, which values the employees. It's the best thing I've ever seen in my sixteen years with the city. It has really pumped up the employees, and we love it. This training money is the best money the city has ever spent."

I sat motionless, in shock, trying not to fall out of my chair, experiencing a City Manager's dream fantasy! When do you ever get praised in public by the union!

As he completed his remarks, I closed my gaping-wide mouth, and my eyes returned to their normal size, back into their respective sockets.

He wrapped up: "Now, I'm going to continue to fight with the City Manager over our contracts because he's been too tight with the pay increases and our need for better benefits over the last two years. But, I just want you to know that you've got a good man there."

Boy, that felt good. But, I never heard a word from the council about it. Why do you think that was?

Lesson: This snapshot is rare. Don't expect it.

Lesson: Too much public praise of the City Manager can impair your political health.

THE CITY MANAGER FISH BOWL

FAME

Along the way, I had fleeting moments of fame, always around problems.

I ended up on the front page of *The Washington Post*, talking about the impact of the regional recession on our community.

In the West, I participated in a seven-minute interview on CBS's *This Morning*. I was interviewed about the negative impact of the first Iraqi war on the economy of our military- base community.

Lesson: Fame is fleeting. I never paid much attention to it unless it affected my paycheck.

Lost Vote

The city councilman approached me after the longish meeting. "What are you going to do about those two policemen who interrupted the charity golf outing yesterday?"

They had investigated a car parked on the eighteenth hole — the prize for a hole in one.

I asked, "What do you mean? What's the problem?"

"They deliberately interrupted that golf outing because they don't like those business people sponsoring the event. They should be disciplined."

I was tired after a tedious budget meeting and replied, a little too strongly, "Look, those guys are down the street right now at the station and worried about whether or not they will have a job because of the complaints about their investigation. The chief reviewed the incident and found nothing wrong. Those folks report to me, and I don't want them worrying about their jobs."

The sixty-seven-year-old councilman responded, with a slightly raised voice, "Yeah, they report to you. But you report to me, and don't you forget it!"

I called him the next day to apologize. He accepted my apology. But, had I lost one vote on the council? Or, maybe the vote was already gone, and I was just now recognizing it.

Months later, he stopped by my house before I left for my next city management position. We laughed, a little, about the incident with mutual apologies.

Lesson: Give diplomacy a priority at all times, especially with elected officials. Be careful when you are tired.

Lesson: Council members insist that the City Manager faithfully convey that he understands who he works for, at all times.

Why We Do Emergency Preparedness

I was City Manager of a community next to a large military base. The president was ready to launch the first Iraqi campaign. School officials were arranging for grief counselors to come in from across the state.

The army had to anticipate that casualties might be high in the coming combat. If so, our community would take a disproportionate hit because so many military families were settled there. It was a very sobering anticipation at a time when the rest of the country was totally at peace and not personally impacted by this upcoming Middle Eastern conflict. My community, however, was immediately in harm's way. I knew these people. They were the backbone of America. It worried me.

Army intelligence advised us of the possibility of international terrorism against the base. They suggested we take precautions. It was good practice anyhow, because who knew what might happen in the future.

I directed the city organization to dust the cobwebs off the old emergency preparedness plans and to update them. We rehearsed emergency exercises.

Three months after I left that city to assume another position, the worst murder rampage in American history, up to that time, took place, with twenty-four dead. A man rammed his vehicle through the window of a popular restaurant. He then calmly walked through the restaurant, executing people.

A Jimmy-Stewart-cowboy-type detective, whom I knew, was the one who ended up responding to the restaurant gunfire scene. He carefully elbow crawled from overturned table to overturned table, exchanging gunfire, until he killed the murderer. He saved lives that day.

Three of the people who were shot, including a personal friend, were saved that day due to the rapid response of city emergency units. Having just practiced for this type of emergency, they were well equipped.

This reminded me again that what we do in this day-to-day business of local government really can be important.

I took the incident personally for another reason as well. My wife liked to go to that restaurant.

WE KNOW THEY'RE DIRTY!

I had never crossed this bridge before. Did I really have to? Wasn't there another option?

After our third wearying conversation, the city attorney, the police chief, and I concluded it was time to go to the district attorney. We strongly suspected two councilmen of selling out the city to a large shopping center interest that we believed owed the city nearly one million dollars.

I had to hand it to these guys. At least they didn't deal in chump change. We also knew that they were actively undercutting the city's franchise renewal negotiations with the cable company. Again, millions of city revenues were at stake. And, there were rumors of other underhanded deals involving waste collection. We did not have hard evidence, but knew enough to request that the DA look into it. We did not want to be viewed down the road as being negligent or accessories after the fact.

The city attorney and police chief went downtown to meet with the DA, separately, on different occasions. Finally, the word came back from the district attorney's office: (1) we know they're dirty; (2) the take is under $100,000; (3) our plate is too full.

Thirty days later, one of the two councilmen sent word back that he knew what we had done. He had friends in the DA's office.

Lesson: Before you go to an outside agency on suspected wrongdoing by an elected official, be sure you have thought it through and there is a convincing case to be made.

In this instance, we had come to the conclusion that we had no choice. We had too much information to ignore the matter, but knew we did not have a "smoking gun" either.

CAUGHT IN THE MIDDLE

I asked the police chief the next day why he had hurriedly approached the council dais at the end of the meeting the previous night.

I had been standing between the mayor and one of the councilmen, while they argued about some minor agenda item. The exchange between the two was heated. I was trying to stay out of it, literally with my head down.

The chief answered, "Didn't you see that the mayor had his fist balled up and was ready to swing at the councilman?"

I wonder if that is a parable for an aspect of this business — getting caught in the middle.

Lesson: Try to not get caught in the middle.

THAT 3:30 AM PHONE CALL

The phone rang at 3:30 AM. It was the police chief, briefing me on a tragic emergency. There had been a combined city, county, FBI stakeout for a dangerous fugitive. The stakeout location was based on information from his girlfriend.

Somehow, the fugitive became alerted to the stakeout. He snuck up behind the FBI agent's car and shot him twice in the back of the head.

A running gun battle ensued. Sixty-six shots were exchanged. The fugitive shot and killed himself behind a Dumpster.

I rose from bed, dressed quickly, and went to the scene. There was nothing for me to do, but I needed to be there, out of respect for the dead FBI agent, if nothing else.

After visiting the scene and getting briefed by the police chief, I went home and called the Council.

The combined police unit went to the fugitive's apartment, where his best friend was staying. The officers were upset. They overreacted; a boot print was still visible on the friend's back forty-eight hours later, among other signs of maltreatment.

The news story the following day was on the front page and lengthy. There were two paragraphs about the dead FBI agent and his wife and their three young children, left fatherless. I read about the boot print, knew it was wrong, didn't care.

In the following months, the newspaper printed conspicu-ous stories about the police brutality, with pictures, and the civil rights lawsuits. There was never another mention of the dead FBI agent and his family.

CITY MANAGERS TALK CANDIDLY ABOUT DYSFUNCTIONAL POLITICAL PROBLEMS IN LOCAL GOVERNMENT

AND I THOUGHT
I HAD TROUBLE!

So, there I was, having a beer with a colleague at the annual International City Management Association Conference welcoming reception in Fort Worth, Texas. He and I had become good friends years earlier when we were competing finalists for a City Manager job in Colorado.

Back then, having toured the city together before the council interview, we both agreed we didn't want the job. So, we decided to ask the council for more money than they were willing to pay. It worked. Neither of us got the job. Brilliant work!

Slowly sipping my beer, I started whining about how my city council has turned over in the recent election, with new members, and the trouble I was having.

My ICMA colleague turned to his friend and introduced me to Hector. Hector was Hispanic, stood five foot six, and weighed 135 pounds. He had been City Manager of a city that bordered Mexico. "Hector, tell him your story. Listen to this."

Hector answered the door one Saturday night. The police chief stood there awkwardly, an embarrassed look on his face, stuttering, hemming and hawing.

Finally, Hector said, "Chief, what's going on? Spit it out!"

The chief blurted out, "I have to get you and your family to the airport and out of town right away! A contract has been put out on you by the local drug dealer, in retaliation for you telling me to clean up the town."

The City Manager put his family on the next plane to the Northeast, where they had relatives. Hector started carrying a gun because he was scared. Searching desperately for help, Hector remembered a classmate of his from Harvard who was now with the U.S. Drug Enforcement Administration.

Would his classmate remember him? Would he help?

Hector made the phone call. Within days, two hundred agents flooded the area. Message sent.

A month later, Hector was stopped by a county officer at night and given a traffic citation. Totally out of the ordinary, he was arrested and taken to jail for this issued citation.

He spent the night in the county lockup. Only after he called his lawyer the next day was he released and able to appear before the judge. The judge lectured him on the seriousness of the traffic violation. This was puzzling. Then, it started to make sense. Message sent. The tentacles of the drug business had a long reach.

Hector, a man of courage, but also with a family and common sense, left the city six months later.

Hearing the story, my whining stopped, for a time. After the conference I went back to my city with renewed energy and more perspective.

DRUG RUNNING?

The midwestern police chief was high profile and respected in the region. I approached my relationship with him cautiously. Many places, I found, the police chief was the best politician in town and the most powerful. I wanted to get that relationship right because I've always had great respect for the work of the folks in blue.

The more I worked with the chief, the better I liked him. He exhibited characteristics of the old school (respect for superiors, executed his job by the numbers, valued law and order) and attributes of the new school (excellent public relations, advocacy for technology, sincere commitment to civil rights). Oh, yes, the most important ingredient: backbone for doing the right thing.

In most of my City Manager assignments, I had been blessed with excellent police chiefs, and he was another one. A good police chief saves the City Manager from a lot of headaches. Usually 50 percent of the city's personnel problems and its litigation originate in the police department. The potential legal liability of the department, given the nature of the work, is enormous.

This chief exhibited seasoned judgment and excellent administrative skills. He'd been police chief for years. He was White, conservative, Protestant, and Republican. Why I note that, you'll see.

He continued to wrestle, as I did, with successfully integrating the practically all-White organization that was only fifteen minutes away from one of the larger Black populations in the country.

The civil rights agenda represented more than doing the right thing. Integration was smart business. With integration, the organization and his department could be more effective in dealing with an increasingly diverse community. Like me, the chief realized that a salt-and-pepper police force offered more personal safety for the street cops too: less likelihood of someone overreacting on either side in a street-stop dispute.

He had taken over the police chief's chair fifteen years earlier. Commenting on the historical organizational resistance to change, he said things were good for him, now. But, they were rough there, for a while, in the beginning, especially with some counterproductive staff he inherited.

I asked, "How many years was it a tough go before you got things straightened out?"

He responded, "Twelve or thirteen years."

I paused for a long, long time. No wonder I was viewed as making too many waves in my short time there.

Before becoming chief, he spent his first career coming up through the ranks in the nearby large, urban city police department with a significant Black population. Assigned to the mayor's office, he thought he saw some things he wasn't supposed to see (drug use in the mayor's office) but kept his mouth shut. Maybe he hadn't seen what he thought.

In his large, urban police department, working with vice, he and his fellow officers surfaced actionable intelligence to do significant drug busts in the late 1960s and the 1970s.

Numerous times, right before his unit was ready to take down the bad guys, they were directed by the feds to step back and let it go. While there was always the possibility of a bigger picture, such as a federal sting in the works, the chief didn't see it that way. He never saw any subsequent, larger case emerge. Drugs flooded the city.

He became convinced the CIA used the drug flow to pacify the inner cities. The inner cities had gone up in flames, from civil insurrections, years earlier.

Illicit drug revenues were off the books and could be used to support untraceable activities. Sounded like the makings of a spy thriller movie. He said he had no first-hand evidence.

We were just talking, shooting the breeze.

My intuition whispered he owned specifics and information beyond what he was telling me that led him to this conclusion, stuff that was really too hot to handle.

I didn't press him. I didn't want to know. No longer young and foolhardy, I didn't see this as exciting stuff. It was all too possible, as later post-Vietnam era revelations became public.

This police chief was the last person in the world I expected to lay out a CIA conspiracy theory and accuse his government of dirty dealing.

I was right to doubt him, wasn't I?

WE'RE BEING FOLLOWED!

The mayor stopped in. Something was on his mind.

He feared that city police were following his daughter, his wife, and a couple of in-laws. Another member of the council had the same concern.

The mayor didn't have hard proof. But, the specific instances he cited of police seemingly following folks were highly unusual and mildly convincing.

The town was racked with class division: the bourgeois small business owner/council members versus the union/blue collar/ populist council members. It was the worst class division I had ever seen, and it ran deep.

The previous mayor said about his council member colleague, "I went to high school with her thirty years ago. She was dumb then, and she's dumb now." That captured the depth of the political chasm.

Even though I personally despised the current mayor, and I knew it was mutual, I respected his elected position and was outraged that we could be experiencing police state tactics.

Was it true? How to handle?

I wanted to show the mayor that I was fair and respected his concern. I prepared to follow up on the matter, even though he and I stood far apart on most issues.

When I brought the police chief into my confidence, I received a guarded, noncommittal response without enthusiasm. It seemed to fit my experiences with him, such as previously attending the police union dinner and going over to his table to sit with him and sensing his reluctance to be seen with me.

The chief said he'd look into it but probably wouldn't find much. He didn't find much.

Two days later, I broached the subject again with the police chief. Out of our conversation of options evolved his suggestion of retaining an ex-FBI agent in the area to do an investigation and give us a report.

It seemed to make sense. The agent possessed the needed experience and would be discreet. If word got out, it would send the right messages. After all, this wasn't just some private detective; this guy had been FBI.

The informal, professional probe would tell the mayor I was committed to fairness over politics. It would tell any rogue cops to knock it off.

I retained the ex-agent. He did his job. He interviewed several officers on specific beats and times related to the allegations. He issued his report. There was nothing definitive.

It all blew up. Someone selectively leaked the allegations and the inquiry to the newspaper, with political spin. The front page story did not herald the dedicated City Manager, committed to truth, justice, and the American way. It was about a paranoid mayor and a councilman seeing bogeymen everywhere.

I could tell that the humiliated mayor blamed me, although he didn't say anything. I wish he had. The police chief, with whom I had developed this option, wasn't weighing in. In city-manager-speak, he was MIA when he was needed. This had clearly been my decision.

On Saturday night, I received a phone call from a City Manager colleague in the city next door. He said his wife worked at the local newspaper. He wanted to give me a discreet heads-up.

The newspaper would be carrying a full page a
ing sponsored by the police union attacking me fo
the police surveillance allegations. The union woul
agent's inconclusive findings as proof that nothing ___...

I appreciated the call. It gave me a chance to call the mayor and each council member that evening to do some damage control before the paper hit the streets.

Several weeks after this, the mayor's councilman friend, who also thought he had been followed, was arrested for drunk driving.

He had left the hotel bar and nearly hit three police cars parked a block away. Why were three police cars parked there? I later heard they knew where his watering hole was.

Then, while I was out of town at an ICMA conference, video clips of the councilman in the drunk tank made it onto the TV news, supposedly at the initiation of Mothers Against Drunk Driving. I never did get a good explanation of how they secured the film footage.

The council member's drunk driving was wrong, but he was a decent guy. He had started drinking heavily after his wife died a year earlier. The TV coverage of him in the drunk tank totally humiliated him.

I left that city several months later.

Three weeks into my new City Manager job, a councilman pulled me aside and said the council had received a letter from the police union of my former city. The police union had urged them to not hire me because I was not friendly to the police. Amused, the councilman said that the letter arrived one week after I had been hired.

I was not amused.

He further advised that he and the rest of the council were glad that I was tough enough to stand up to foolishness. They didn't like the feeling of being pushed around by the boys in blue.

During the whole police allegation matter, I never felt certainty about what may have really happened. However, in the new job, a year later, I intuitively concluded that the police were following the people. Sometimes, you just know; although it took me a while.

Lesson: Get as much pertinent information as you can before you make a decision on a tough issue.

Lesson: Consult with someone you can trust, at least to bounce ideas off of. I did not have that in this instance.

Lesson: Many times City Managers are in a tough spot. Be as smart, as diplomatic, as hard-working as you can, but you may still end up the creek without the necessary paddle.

Lesson: Make sure you know how to swim in political waters.

Of Course They're Listening In!

Handsome, intelligent, president of the class at our undergraduate alma mater, he went to work on Capitol Hill, right after Georgetown Law School. With his talent and ambition, he ended up staffing the Senate Watergate Committee, investigating Nixon's misdeeds.

My job moved me also to Washington right at the time of Watergate. A cadre of our alma mater grads had relocated there.

I called him to see if he wanted to play poker with us. We usually met once a month, and he had sat in twice before. The poker group liked me and him because we were easy money. We played with more enthusiasm than skill.

I thought he might be too busy right now, with the Watergate Hearings on television every day, but I still wanted to check in with him. I needed him at the table because he was a worse poker player than me.

Laughing, I opened my telephone call to him, "Hey, man, are we being tapped by the CIA?"

No response; and a concerned, chilled no response it was. I felt like an idiot.

Of course his phone was under surveillance.

Did I embarrass him?

BEING SPIED ON

I was City Manager of the Washington DC suburb and was asked to host a one-week internship for a local government official who was part of a delegation from Russia. The Soviet Empire had imploded and Russia was picking up the pieces.

In his late twenties, the Russian intern was a public information officer for a large city 250 miles north of Moscow. He could have been the blond-haired, blue-eyed poster child for the defunct Young Pioneers.

He was so totally engaging that my wife and I provided him with a suitcase full of our children's former baby clothes, since his wife was expecting their first child, a girl.

Our children's clothes, purchased from high-end American stores because my daughters had to have the best, according to their mom, were worth a fortune at that time back in Russia. He wrote back from Russia to thank us when his daughter was born.

The day after he left, the police chief called to say that the FBI had had all of the Russian interns under surveillance, since they were believed to be KGB agents. My first reaction was anger and a sense of betrayal.

Then I asked myself, what had they seen?

Well, they had received a complete tour of the NASA facility right next door to us. We had also shown them how we live and how we think: our schools, churches, shopping centers, and our homes.

After more thought, I concluded it was good to have shown them everything. I had been to the Communist East eleven years earlier and had seen that nothing worked or functioned properly. I wanted them to see everything in this country and take it back home. That way the new KGB, or whoever was running the show under a new name, would realistically know what they were up against and how strong this country really is, despite our publicized problems.

They'd better worry about the Chinese instead of trying to take us on again.

PARANOID POLITICIANS

Standing outside the conference room before the evening meeting, I asked, "Mayor, may I borrow your key? I locked myself out of my office."

Three days later while working in my office on Saturday morning, the phone rang. It was the mayor.

"I thought I'd find you there working. You are a liar. You didn't lose your key. You wanted to see if I could get in the city offices with my key. You wanted to see if I had anything to do with the recent embezzlement in the finance department. And, I noticed the funny look on your face."

I responded, "Mayor, the funny look was because I was embarrassed to have locked myself out, and I felt foolish asking you to let me in. And, no, you are not a suspect in the embezzlement and never have been."

This was a different city and a different mayor from the one where the police were suspected of trailing the elected officials and their families. Paranoia must be part of the job description for some people.

THE LOCAL PRESS EXAMINES THE NEW CITY MANAGER

D HARMAN

The Fourth Estate—What A Disappointment!

My biggest problem with the press over the years stemmed from reporters not digging deep enough to find the story behind the story and not shining enough sun where it needed to shine.

"See no evil."

In one city, the press didn't seem to want to investigate what was really going on with the development projects. The city hall grapevine whispered that businessmen had threatened to withhold auto dealer sales ads if the local press got too rambunctious. I really couldn't do much about these questionable development deals, unless they were downright illegal.

But it was never blatant illegality; that would be amateurish. The proposed development deals always made exceptions in favor of the prominent, local developer, overriding city staff's recommendations.

In this same city, the mayor suggested I look for an opportunity to do a downtown development deal with J. T., a long-time friend who ran a small store downtown.

Urban legend had it that J. T. had been the bagman for the community businesses years ago. When the community needed a federal dam, they collected fifty thousand dollars, which was the going rate at the time. J. T. was supposed to deliver it to the vice president. (The vice-president of what, you ask? You know.) The complaint came back that only forty thousand arrived in Washington. They didn't use J. T. again.

Fact or fiction? I had my opinion. After all, there was a federal dam nearby.

"Determined to be adversaries"

I have always been an advocate for a strong, free press and open government. In fact, I authored a professional journal article noting techniques to support open government. It referenced ways to build relations with the media and keep an open door. Over the years, I observed veteran City Managers with cynical, negative attitudes toward the press. That wasn't me.

So, wearing my open government philosophy on my sleeve, I made it a point to visit the local newspaper publisher during my second week on the job in the friendly city. I heard that the publisher was bright and energetic, a graduate of one of the best schools in the country. City staff advised that my City Manager predecessor and the publisher had been good friends in the past, and then the friendship cooled in recent years.

I extended myself, hoping to make a good impression. I reaffirmed my commitment to open government and reaching out to keep the news media informed. I reported that I had established a public affairs officer (PAO) position in my last city, just to meet the information needs of the media.

Halfway through our conversation, the publisher commented that he thought the relationship between his newspaper and city hall should be adversarial.

Puzzled, I responded by saying surely he meant "dynamic," or "critical," or "skeptical."

Nope. He meant adversarial. I thought that was unfair, a pre-judgment. How could he practice balanced journalism that way?

In that city, I soon budgeted a PAO. The same publisher took great offense. He believed that the PAO position unfairly helped his two regional newspaper competitors, who were not as historically and locally based as he was, even though one of the competitors had located in an office in our downtown.

One Saturday night, I received an unexpected, flaming e-mail from the local publisher. He said that if I wanted war, then it was time to take the gloves off! Greatly concerned, I responded within minutes, asking for an immediate meeting early in the week to find out what had upset him so much.

I figured I had screwed up badly to warrant such anger on his part.

Several days later at our meeting, he described his outrage. He had to explain it to me twice, because I couldn't believe what I was hearing the first time. It infuriated him to see my jaw literally drop in disbelief. "I knew that would be your reaction!" he shouted.

The city's PAO had issued a press release to the three newspapers late Friday afternoon. The press release announced the death that day of a previous mayor of our city. By issuing this press release, according to the publisher, we had removed the hometown advantage his newspaper should have enjoyed. He wanted badly to scoop this story and had been in contact the week prior with the mayor's family. He accused us of subsidizing the other newspapers with local tax dollars.

I was appalled. Stunned and mute, I couldn't put words together. I opened my mouth and nothing came out; twice. This further outraged him.

I decided to leave the meeting as soon as I could, especially after he launched a personal tirade against the PAO who had accompanied me.

We were definitely "guilty" of honoring the memory and contributions of a beloved former mayor. We were also guilty of treating all three papers the same, providing the press release simultaneously.

Worse, I had no apologies for it. I told him we would do it again, when the inevitable and unfortunate circumstance occurred of losing a beloved elected official.

Within weeks of the encounter, someone e-mailed this same newspaper with a bomb threat against the local high school. The press immediately referred it to the school, who contacted our police department.

The police asked the press for immediate access to the newspaper's computer and the e-mail address of the person who made the threat. They were refused by the newspaper. Instead, the publisher required the police to get a subpoena. This cost the police investigator six hours of lost time.

The paper's insistence on the subpoena was not about protecting some theoretical informant or whistle-blower who might be at risk. This was shielding the criminal himself. There were potentially serious consequences for delay.

The misjudgment of the publisher was blasted the next day by a competing newspaper. The headlines quoted the police chief's upset.

Then, the same publisher who mishandled the bomb threat, angered at the negative competing coverage, called the reporter at the other paper, yelling and berating him for twenty minutes. (Where was the management of that paper while this was going on?)

Sensing community anger over the handling of the issue, or, responding to the police chief's newspaper phraseology referencing "aiding and abetting," the publisher and his editor scheduled a meeting the next day with the police chief.

I walked into the meeting unannounced. The newspaper team was surprised and not happy to see me. An understanding was reached that if there was a next time, they would voluntarily be a help and not a hindrance to public safety.

During the same time period, this newspaper sued one of the city council members, demanding access to the private e-mails on the elected official's private computer. They believed the newspaper was entitled to view the private e-mails, even though it was sent on a personal computer, because the council member had discussed *city business.*

The attorney retained by the newspaper for the law suit was the spouse of the unsuccessful mayoral candidate from six months earlier. As you might have guessed, that unsuccessful candidate had been endorsed by the same newspaper against the city hall favorite son.

On top of all of this, the following ad for this newspaper appeared on the web for the vacant city hall beat reporter position:

> The job is made tougher by the sometimes tense relationship with the city, thanks in part to a yet-to-be resolved lawsuit the paper filed over access to a council member's e-mails, and a city manager with a bent toward propaganda.

"You contributed to his death"

In the larger city, I strategically created a public affairs office to deal with the very aggressive media. The lazy electronic media created their daily TV and radio stories from the daily newspaper.

Some in city hall snickered that it was the best weekly newspaper around, printed on a daily basis. The newspaper tended to run the same key story, with variations, for several days. It was also the only paper in town.

Despite everyone's complaints about the sensationalist liberal tone and coverage, the newspaper was massively influential. Everyone, including myself, who criticized them, also quoted them. Their reporting reached a population area of over 1.5

million. I could go to the mountains and see my name in a story. I would go to the beach and see my name in a story.

They could hurt people. Sometimes the people deserved it; sometimes they didn't. If you were in the public eye, you were fair game. Looking back, I am surprised that with all of the political controversy over the years I was there, I wasn't crucified a number of times. I was rarely praised, either. In that community, the real high-profile players were the mayor and the police chief.

I had appointed the police chief from within the department. It was controversial. He had gotten off the straight and narrow years ago as a young officer, for a period, and then rebounded.

When I was considering his appointment, I had an outside police expert do an assessment. The report came back: this guy was one of the best of over three hundred police chief candidates the consultant had seen in over thirty years.

The assessment proved 100 percent accurate. Appointing him was one of the best decisions I ever made. Turning him loose and supporting him was the second best decision. After three years of his leadership, Part I crime (murder, rape, robberies) had dropped to its lowest in thirty-three years.

The reporter who covered the police chief's appointment was relentless, looking for personal scandals. Many considered the reporter vindictive. (Near the end of my tenure, I refused to speak to him.)

He had tried to dig up as much dirt as he could to derail the police chief's appointment; and there was stuff to dig up. But, this old news of sins committed was already known by the community. The police chief candidate spoke regularly at his church about his past and the power of redemption.

The reporter could never prevail upon anyone to corroborate the rumors and hearsay. He couldn't get over that.

After several years, tragedy struck two weeks before Christmas. An Hispanic police lieutenant committed suicide two hundred feet from the police chief's house. The chief wasn't at home. The lieutenant and the chief had been friends for twenty-three years; they also served together on the SWAT team when they were young.

The lieutenant was under investigation for alleged improprieties with female personnel within the department. It was a problem because of his supervisory rank. The lieutenant felt under enormous pressure because he dreaded that the press would drag his name through the mud, tearing his family apart.

The press dug into the suicide story with the vindictive reporter assigned, because at the same time, it surfaced that a White police captain was having an affair with an employee in city hall, but not a police employee. The employee happened to be the executive assistant to the City Manager—my assistant. The press had been waiting to see if the two situations would be treated the same: Hispanic lieutenant and White captain.

While the two situations might look similar, they weren't. One involved alleged supervisor/subordinate issues; the other was private, between two adults. Both situations were obviously ethically wrong.

The news coverage was atrocious. At one point, a news story by the vindictive reporter, twisting the words of the widow out of context, hinted that the police chief may have murdered his friend.

The coverage also went into as much detail as the newspaper could get on the affair between my staffer and the police captain. The newspaper treated her like a public official—even though she wasn't—and put a private, consensual matter out on the table for everyone to dissect. It included newspaper statements of outrage by her husband against city officials for *allowing* this to happen.

Of course, when the front page story hit, the article deliberately mentioned six times, "the executive assistant to the City

Manager," even when it wasn't necessary. Everyone understood after the first two mentions.

Shortly thereafter, I attended a newspaper editorial board meeting with the mayor and a couple of staff to discuss various city initiatives. At the end, the other city staff and the mayor seemed to leave the room quickly. While I was loading up the briefcase to leave, a couple of questions came up from the editorial board about these affairs.

(I did not know then that this was a favorite press ambush technique. The meeting is over, and just one or two additional questions come up. Or, you are at the door, and you hear, "Oh, by the way, did...")

Was the disciplinary handling equitable in both cases? I responded accurately on point and then cut loose: "I know you have a job to do. I have always respected that. But you have control over how you do your job. You people need to look within yourselves and ask if you contributed to the suicide and the ruining of people's lives. The lieutenant was wrong if he engaged in affairs with subordinates, but he was also loved and respected for a lifetime of public safety service.

"Did his fear of what you were going to do to him cause him to kill himself? I think it did. You all live with that. As for my executive assistant, she is not a public official. And while the affair was wrong, and I do not condone it, it is not a business matter."

I began to walk out. The editor halted me, saying, "So, you're just going to lecture us and walk out?"

"You bet," I responded.

"Cynical City Manager"

I had always carried a glamorized view of the press.

Early in my career, I worked in the same jurisdiction that Bob Woodward covered, right before he moved to *The Washington*

Post and the Watergate story. Unfortunately, the next generations of reporters were hell-bent on finding Watergate in all of our city halls, on every news story.

An older and wiser City Manager reminded me years ago that the press was nothing more than a corporation set up to make money through advertising. No one elected them. No one anointed them. Their self-righteousness and smugness were not deserved, nor were they earned.

Lesson: Forget Woodward and Bernstein.

Lesson: None of the media are owned by non-profits. They are there to make money; that's mission # 1.

Lesson: The media are not your friends.

Lesson: For the media, it's not always about what the truth is, but rather how can the story be presented for maximum impact.

Lesson: If it bleeds, it leads.

Final Lesson: There is no more Sergeant Joe Friday from *Dragnet* saying, "Just the facts, ma'am."

What Do Heroes Look Like? And, What Makes Them Heroes?

In my youth, my heroes were religious and sports figures, larger than life. There was also my father, who fought on both the Japanese and German fronts in World War Two, and my uncles, one shot down and killed flying over Germany and the other one shot up at the bridge at Remagen. (Remember the movie about the bridge the Germans didn't blow up? In real life my uncle was the seventh soldier across the bridge that day.)

As I got older, some of my heroes were political figures, which is probably why I went into the city management business. They appeared dauntless and were people of great accomplishment.

Now that I've kicked around a bit and have some gray hair to prove it, I still believe in heroes, but they look different than they used to. Let me tell you about some of the ones I've met in the cities I've served in.

Two police officers, at immediate risk to themselves, rescued the victim of a hit-and-run from his burning vehicle. To them, it was probably just another day, with a little excitement thrown in to break up the monotony of routine patrol.

In August of 1992, a city police dispatcher volunteered to go to Florida and assist the homeless and hungry in the aftermath of Hurricane Andrew. Three weeks in Florida, in August, after complete devastation, is not vacation-land.

Two public works employees were at the scene of a burning, crashed airplane on a neighborhood street. They alerted the occupants of the nearby house to evacuate in case of another explosion. They then, at personal risk, got a garden hose to douse the flames and attempted a rescue of the pilot and passenger.

A city recreation supervisor adopted two children from orphanages in Russia—an expensive enterprise. This means a lifetime of commitment and worry and anxiety about these two new little ones in her life. But, think what this adoption means to these children who will have a totally different life from living in Russia.

The public works director tutored a high school student every week. His student went from a "D" grade to an "A."

In what could have easily been just a routine investigation, two police officers made an extra effort and recovered what turned out to be a stolen vehicle. As a result, the officers rescued a pictorial autobiography on diskette from the car.

This diskette was left for a ten-year-old son by his terminally ill mother. The mother had died before making a copy of the diskette. Because of the diligence of these two officers, a child who lost his mother will now be able to keep his memories of her alive forever.

In her private time, the personnel officer regularly worked with community members to find emergency assistance or shelter for people in dire straits.

I especially liked the part when she had been lied to or the money was totally misused by the person in need. She and the staff would be down in the dumps for about five minutes and then bounce right back, ready to help someone else again.

How about those public works guys keeping the roads open at 3:00 AM in the worst winter weather we have ever seen! Yes, I know they get overtime pay for it, but I'd rather be safe and warm in my bed, not sliding around in a salt truck.

In one city, a police sergeant quickly surmised the likely escape route and apprehended nine suspects considered armed and dangerous in the murder of a thirteen-year-old altar boy.

He held the suspects until backup arrived, who assisted with the arrests and recovered the murder weapon. The officer attributed the action to "good teamwork, and I was lucky."

I want to put in a good word about my former bosses, the city councils. These folks have regular full-time jobs and families to look after, and then they contribute many, many additional hours to serving the public. Yes, they do get attention and some pay for that, but they also are subjected to aggravation that you don't see. I've seen them at 11:50 PM struggling to say awake while one of their colleagues or the City Manager drones on.

My City Manager hero, an icon in this profession, uncovered systematic police padding of overtime. He was nervous, because he was accountable, and it was on his watch as City Manager. He informed the council of the wrongdoing. They said forget it. The politically powerful police union, fearing felony charges by the City Manager against many of its members, told the council to fire the City Manager.

The mayor quietly suggested to the City Manager that he take extended sick leave. The City Manager said he wasn't sick.

The Council fired the City Manager, refusing to honor his contract providing for severance.

It took three years of over fifty depositions and court appearances, but after putting all of his assets on the line and his career on hold, the City Manager won a one-million-dollar settlement, plus back benefits.

I hired that City Manager some time after these events. I needed interim help. I also wanted to politically rehabilitate him, because many looked at him askance for having taken strong legal action.

It worked. He has a successful consultant business. He's a little sour on the profession. I understand.

I had persuaded a retired, brilliant City Manager to come in and help me out on an interim basis in the big, challenging city. The temporary assignment lasted for three years and five executive positions. His experienced, competent performance saved my job at least once. He was taking sixteen pills a day for serious health problems. Unknown to anyone, he donated his salary from the interim assignments to his church.

Years ago I had the good fortune to tell another City Manager colleague that he was a hero of mine. Now, since I told him that in the men's room as we were washing our hands at the sink, he may have thought I was kidding.

But, I wasn't.

He was an exceedingly bright and accomplished man. He lost his wife to cancer and had two young kids to raise. He then fought cancer himself. Meanwhile, he was facing an attack back home from his city council...some political horse puckey.

I was undergoing "transition" (city-manager-speak for "fired"), and this guy calls me to see how I'm doing?

I wasn't doing well, and I greatly appreciated the call. He had moved into retirement, doing consulting and writing. I could hear his kids, teenagers by then, yelling in the background; he yelled back at them to quiet down. That's real family life, not the Norman Rockwell painting of everyone sitting around the dinner table, holding hands, and smiling at one another. I know there's a lot of genuine family love where he lives.

Thanks for the call.

Then there was the little hero, my seven-year-old daughter who befriended her classmate. He was lonely because his mother was in jail in another state, and his father worked all day.

My contribution had been to tell the boy to stop calling so much or to tell him it's late and he needs to go home. He was a good, gentle boy. I should have had my eyes and ears open and been more supportive. Shame on me.

It's amazing what you can see when you pay attention and look around.

What do your heroes look like?

Lesson: Keep your eyes open for heroes.

Thanks, Sam

Many of us in city management ended up there for reasons we may not understand for years.

As a ten-year-old, I developed a respect for public service from an unusual source, my baseball coach. I didn't fully recognize this until later years when I presented remarks at a police officer swearing-in ceremony. I reflected on why I see police in the positive way that I do.

As a Little Leaguer, baseball obsessed me. I was a good, but not great, player. I augmented my mediocre skills with hard work, dedication, and enthusiasm. (That was the City Manager career stratagem I utilized as well.) Others on the team also gave their best because we had the greatest coach in the world, Sam Dooley.

By day, Sam was coach of our first-place-winning team. We practiced three times a week at 9:00 AM, no matter how hot it was.

By night, Sam was a cop patrolling a tough town.

As the summer wore on, I realized that Officer Dooley often came to our practices looking tired and needing a shave. He worked the 11:00 PM to 7:00 AM shift. He ran all night, chasing bad guys. Then, he showed up at practice, giving us 100 percent of his fired-up coaching talent. Occasionally, he showed up with cuts and bruises. You know what that was about.

I was impressed with this at age ten, especially when Officer Dooley coached us to the championship. It wasn't until I was much older that I understood and appreciated his sacrifices even more. To me, all police officers were, and are, Sam Dooleys.

Fairly or not, that's what I've always looked for in our city employees.

Because of that perspective, it takes me to the next snapshot...

JUST SEND THEM A CHECK

In job interviews, I describe myself as "friendly, fair, and firm," committed to inspiring our employees to reach their full potential but ready to take personnel action when required.

I declare to receptive and unreceptive political listeners, that I take more pride in fixing, not firing, people.

That said, over the years, I began to understand a personnel phenomenon no one had referenced in the textbooks: the counterproductive employee. We all acknowledge the sad stereotype of the lackluster, let's-just-get-by civil servant. But, this counterproductive employee is in its own specially awful category. This employee compels descriptions beyond "complacent."

"Toxic" is more apropos.

This cancerous organizational presence uncoils itself in about 1 percent of the work force. It would literally be better for the organization if these employee were to sit at home and receive their paycheck—anything to keep them away from the workplace.

They spend all their time at the workplace undercutting their boss, fighting with colleagues, complaining continually, and badmouthing the organization.

If there's a way to create mischief, they will. It really becomes scary when, in addition to their attitude, they don't even know what they are doing and are totally self-righteous in their actions, or in their ignorance.

They are: wronged, abused, misled, not appreciated, denied a promotion, underpaid, angry, overworked, at risk, not receiving proper direction, no one tells them what is going on, and unhappy. The list goes on.

This type of public sector employee can hide behind too many protective shields that were initially put there to protect against abuse, patronage, favoritism, and discrimination. With the constraining provisions of union contracts thrown in the mix, he or she has burrowed deep into the organizational immunities.

The "counterproductives" are expert in union contracts and personnel provisions, knowing them better than the human resources department professionals. To try to remove them expeditiously triggers a major project in itself, which is a distraction from the established organizational workload. Too early removal can even jeopardize your own employment when you justifiably intervene.

In a city where I was a department head, I inherited a rather dysfunctional unit. (In fact, this was my inheritance in more than one city.)

Between meetings in a conversational aside with the City Manager, I mentioned observing seriously negative behavior by one of my department supervisors. Complaints by department personnel had been previously filed against her.

The City Manager said, "Fire her."

"Well, I'm not sure I have sufficient grounds yet. I just wanted you to know I'm paying attention to it," I replied.

I knew terminations required careful handling. Even in cut-and-dried cases, there were usually attorneys hired by the dismissed employee.

"No, just fire her," came the terse response, his standard communication style.

I did not say anything.

I continued to monitor her behavior.

Several weeks later, the employee in question engaged in volatile behavior that compelled me to send her home. I had checked with the human resources department, and we touched all the right paperwork bases in sending her home on paid leave.

Weeks later, I recommended that she be terminated. Nothing happened.

Weeks later, I recommended that she be terminated. Nothing happened.

Finally, I recommended the matter be resolved in some fashion. She was sitting at home, still being paid, and nothing was happening.

Five months later, we went into a closed session with the city council to brief them. Several minutes into the briefing by the City Manager and city attorney, one of the council members glared at me and said, "Did he engage in any personal impropriety with the employee?"

"What the hell is this?" I thought. "I'm the one who delayed firing her until the case was a slam dunk, and I was sure it was the right and fair thing to do. Now, I'm under attack?"

The City Manager quickly said, "No. This has nothing to do with him. It's been a problem for some time, before he got here, and he's addressing it." Even with the response, the air remained polluted with the councilman's inquiry.

So, I had gone from director not taking action until all the ducks were lined up, to taking action, to waiting while nothing happened, to all of a sudden having my character questioned.

This turnabout happens too frequently. It makes supervisors reluctant to do their job. It creates mediocre and dysfunctional organizations.

In another city, I had a counterproductive mid-management unit. They blocked effective supervision by the department director, created friction between management and the employees they were supervising, and feathered their own nests at every turn.

After having a reputable outside consultant analyze the situation, I made the decision to reorganize the department and abolish the mid management unit. It was the only way. Otherwise, I would be in individual grievances and mediations until the Second Coming of the Lord.

We followed all the procedures. It took a while, including the addition of a public city council agenda item, but mission accomplished.

I thought I was home free! What brilliant, decisive management!

One of the individuals in the abolished unit was rumored to have been the campaign manager of a sitting councilperson.

There's an old saying in our business: "Friends come and go, but enemies accumulate."

During this period, all of sudden, out of nowhere, a very critical anonymous letter was sent to the local press accusing me of everything from managing by fear and intimidation to liking to talk to pretty girls in the organization. (At least there were no allegations of misbehavior, thank God.)

Of course, excerpts of the letter appeared on the newspaper's front page. This was a tactic that had been used in the same organization several times in prior years against other senior managers there, including the department head and the former City Manager.

I questioned the propriety of printing an anonymous letter on the front page. When I asked the reporter if he would print an anonymous letter praising the City Manager and saying he was a wonderful administrator, he could only respond with a puzzled look.

I suspected phone calls were being made to council members behind my back, as well.

Yes, I did the right thing. It needed to be done. But, I was getting damned tired of paying this kind of price for doing my job!

Lesson: Recognize that every organization has the "counter-productive employee."

Lesson: If you are lucky, this personnel cancer in the organization is only one percent of the workforce.

Lesson: This negative personnel phenomenon must be addressed, but proceed very carefully.

WHY I GET INTO TROUBLE

We call it the art and science of public administration. I deserved high marks for knowing the science: two master's degrees, plus innumerable seminars and readings to stay up on the profession. The art part was trickier.

The big, old, abandoned house squatted ominously across the street from the elementary school, with a weed and trash infested lawn, peeling paint, and a sagging porch. Police responded weekly to reports of vagrants breaking into the house. I drove by the location several times, concerned about the safety of the small children walking to the school across the street. The decrepit house and wasted yard looked scary, forbidding to me. I wasn't seven years old, either.

My charge to staff: make something happen; fine the owners into making repairs, or go through the legal process to tear it down. I supervised a bright, hard-working staff and had high expectations for what they could do because I had seen them in action.

Next month, I ask, "Where are we at?" Reasons are given. We're preparing notices to the owner.

Next month: "Where are we at?" Reasons given. Notices have gone out to the owner.

Next month: "Where are we at?" Owners say they don't have money for repairs.

Month after month.

Finally, in a weekly senior staff meeting, after I asked the status again, one of the staff said, "Well, the city council probably won't like us putting pressure on a private property owner."

I know, in retrospect, I should have said, "Well, let's...," or, "Who wants to take the lead on this? or, Can someone coordinate?" or, "I'll call the council."

Too late; I was incensed. I had been clear on wanting the problem fixed. I thought I was being a good manager by letting staff work out the solution together. Instead, little happened.

I have a no-nonsense look and air, anyhow. Add anger to that, and it's not a recipe for a pretty face. So, I'm sure it was perceived more strongly than intended. I pointed out that if some derelict hiding in the house pulls a little girl in there, then the staff will all move very, very quickly; but it will be way too little, way too late.

"This kind of thing happens," I told the staff.

Get moving. I don't want it happening in my city, on my watch. If something happens, the press will be all over this. Then, there will be no satisfactory excuse.

"Can you see the front page story, 'Homeless Man Drags Little Girl into House'?" I excoriated them. Even me saying that I had staff working on it wouldn't save the day.

Then there would be the lawsuits.

That's not even counting how badly we'd all feel personally.

The problem with my persuasive communication skills is that the person who becomes the most convinced, most quickly, as I talk, is me. So, more wound up, even more sure of the righteousness of my cause, I charge off on my white steed to do battle, banners unfurled.

Then, the very awkward coup de grâce on my part. But remember, I had exercised patience and more patience.

"I would hate to think that we can't get moving on this because it's an Hispanic neighborhood. I don't think this would be tolerated more than one week in my neighborhood or in your neighborhoods."

That was a bridge too far, probably. Staff knew my wife and children were Hispanic, and I leaned forward on Hispanic issues.

An awkward, shocked silence enwrapped the room. I had seized their attention and more.

I either struck right at the heart of the matter, and they had not considered that and were shocked by the thought, or, I was so far off base that I had seriously insulted them.

Maybe I was absent in City Management Class 101 the day the professor covered art. Or, I didn't take very good notes.

Lesson: Choose carefully the occasions and issues for mounting the white steed to sally forth on your crusade. Or, execute your crusade without the white steed, without the trumpets blaring, and without the war banners waving fiercely.

RECOMMENDED READING FOR CITY MANAGERS

孫子兵法

I'M A SHEEPDOG

What! A sheepdog?

An accomplished City Manager colleague, whom I consider a hero in more ways than one, sent me a note calling me a sheepdog. The note included an article by LTC (RET) Dave Grossman, entitled "On Sheep, Wolves and Sheepdogs."

Some excerpts from the article explain:

> Most people are sheep…nothing negative by calling them sheep…they are like the pretty, blue robin's egg…the egg cannot survive without its hard blue shell…police officers, soldiers are like that shell…then there are the wolves… they feed on the sheep without mercy…then there are the sheepdogs…They live to protect the flock and confront the wolf.

> The sheep generally do not like the sheepdog. He looks a lot like the wolf…but he cannot ever harm the sheep…The sheepdog disturbs the sheep. He is a constant reminder that there are wolves in the land…The sheep would much rather have the sheepdog cash in his fangs, spray paint himself white and go, "Baa." Until the wolf shows up.

Understand that there is nothing morally superior about being a sheepdog; it is just what you choose to be…

Sometimes the world of the gray man, the bureaucrat, morphs into political trench warfare, with hand-to-hand combat.

I'm thankful for being called a sheepdog. I hope I have been worthy.

Lesson: We need the sheepdogs.

Commitment To
Good Government

I'm almost embarrassed to mention this for fear I am belaboring the obvious. However, my years in local government have taught me to not take this for granted, and neither should you. *Good government doesn't just happen automatically.*

One local developer exerted influence in city hall to a degree I didn't fully appreciate at the time. Staff told me he commanded connections, but Mr. Integrity, me, didn't fully heed the cautions and had not yet connected the dots.

"Whatrrya, stooopid?" That's what the interim city attorney's *look said.*

She said, "Don't you know that the developer has four of the seven planning commissioners on his payroll, directly or indirectly? The vice-mayor sells the homes that the developer builds. He's in real estate. I know you know *that.*

THE LOOK had changed to "you're crazy."

"And you want to make recommendations against the developer?" she piled on, right after telling me she was resigning to search for another job.

Her predecessor had resigned five months earlier to take a city attorney position in another city. Both were fed up.

"DANGER! Lone Ranger," was what I heard.

This developer frequently appeared before the city council requesting a rezoning, a variance, or an approval of a proposed development. He always demanded some concessions from the city that would benefit his private interest, but not necessarily benefit the community at large.

Because of his connections, I eventually surmised that I was expected to smooth the way to make his requests more palatable for public acceptance and painless council approval.

While I was willing to examine all of his requests on their respective merits, I was not going to roll over. I made my best contribution to good local government under the circumstances.

I experienced difficulty with the council granting his request for turning over a one-third acre of the public golf course so his new development could have a privacy fence. I recommended against it and lost.

I'm sure I was viewed as unreasonable in some business quarters.

I hoped the golfers appreciated my position, although no one spoke up.

Lesson: It's always good to know who works for whom.

Lesson: Never, never underestimate the power and influence of developers, especially when they are hometown boys.

Was It Petty Corruption?

The city council gave me public direction to negotiate development agreements with two local developers in ninety days. The mayor and vice mayor advised me privately to negotiate tough with the developers: "Twist their arms until they scream, then we'll know we've a got a good deal for the city. We know them, and they'll complain to us."

I replied that was fine. I always try to negotiate strongly for the city I serve.

The months went by with no agreements. The developers weren't budging from their initial paltry offer that didn't guarantee the city what they were promising.

It seemed like I was the only one who had done the math. These agreements were worth several billion dollars! No one spoke about it, probably because the numbers were so intimidating.

Still no agreements.

I wanted to go back for more public council direction, or discussion, or a public hearing. The elected officials didn't want to publicly revisit anything in a political environment that included a fierce no-growth advocacy group that was ready to legally pounce.

I agreed with the part of the no-growth agenda that insisted the city should obtain a fair deal and not have to underwrite new development. That would be nothing more than a subsidy to the developers from present and future taxpayers.

One afternoon, I was visited separately by two members of the city council, within one hour of each other. Each council member opened the conversation verbatim: "Why are you negotiating so hard with my developer friend? He has done so much for the community."

This was not the mayor or vice mayor, who were businessmen and friends of the developers and who had urged me to hang tough.

One of the council members who visited had no business experience. What they both had in common was that the one developer they were advocating for had always generously responded to their individual requests for donations to their local charities.

One of the two electeds said, "He always opens his checkbook whenever I ask for help for a community activity. I don't know how he affords it."

There did not appear to be an issue of either council member personally receiving funds; although there were rumors that one had a family member receiving golfing favors.

They later accused me of responding too strongly to them, when I peevishly spelled out where we stood in the stalled negotiations and how I felt the developers were not reciprocating my hard-working attempts to close the deal.

Because I had received an exceptional performance evaluation earlier in the year from the entire city council, and because I was very comfortable with them, I dispensed my candor too forthrightly, which was later represented as "offensive."

I could feel the blood oozing out but couldn't reach the developer knife wounds in my back to stanch the flow.

Six years later, there were still no agreements, and I had been long gone by then.

Lesson: To survive in the city management business, never, ever take the good will of an elected official for granted; and always, always, be careful and respectful.

Get Back Here, Quick!

This was the winter City Manager's state conference in pleasantly warm Palm Springs. The hotel projected a casual, upscale ambiance with a teak check-in desk and marble floors. Everyone wore short sleeves. There were no suits in sight. I was going to enjoy the next three days.

Preparing to call room service, the phone rang. Who could be calling? The Assistant City Manager had everything covered back home.

It was the city attorney and panic filled her voice. "Ben, you have to get ahold of Councilman R. right away. They've scheduled an emergency meeting for tomorrow night, and they're going to fire me. You're next. R. doesn't realize what he's doing. He's playing right into their hands."

I promised to call Councilman R. and made a number of calls. No one answered. I called the city attorney back. She pleaded with me to come back to the city.

Good-bye, sunshine.

Good-bye, putting on the practice green.

Good-bye, drinking and exchanging war stories with colleagues.

Good-bye, Palm Springs.

I agreed to return. I still couldn't make the phone connection to R. back home.

I went back to the city the next day and made a beeline to the school where R.'s wife taught. My kids went to the same school. I wanted to convince her of the political "trap" being set for her councilman husband by his two political enemies on the council. I believed she would listen to me.

She wasn't at the school that day. The premonition struck me at precisely the moment of my failed visit. Missing this connection was going to be significant.

It was.

The emergency council meeting that night produced newspaper headlines the next day. Amid charges and countercharges, the city attorney was terminated. It was so politically controversial, with hurled newspaper allegations, that Councilman R. lost his later bid for reelection.

With the loss of R.'s seat, the council majority swung a bad way. It had been a trap all along.

With fortuitous timing I have witnessed few times in my life, the day after the election, I announced that I was taking a City Manager job in another city.

Don't Go Home
The Same Way

I performed my weekly routine, checking in by phone with the individual council members. Somehow, in the course of the conversation, the councilman commented that he always checks his rearview mirror and never goes home exactly the same way: "Can't be too careful, you know."

I remembered that a couple of his council colleagues had quietly passed the word and boycotted him out of his modest, post-retirement business after he started challenging how things worked in the class-divided community.

Given the local politics, he advised me to be cautious, to always slightly change driving routes to work. His advice unsettled me because he was a strong, outspoken supporter of mine, and he had been a former military officer. There was no intent to make me nervous, just a helpful hint.

Talking to another member of council the same afternoon, another City Manager supporter, I mentioned the advice I had received, still slightly disbelieving.

She not only endorsed his advice but elaborated. She counseled that the going rate for a contract on someone was ten thousand dollars around there and that I should be careful. Because of our geographical location, that activity was not unheard of.

I was unnerved. Although I didn't really feel immediate danger, I did call my brother-in-law back in Washington and told him what was going on. He was connected with the Justice Department and other folks.

I didn't want to be dramatic about it. I tried to make light of it but said that if something did happen to me, to have it checked out—for the sake of my wife and two small daughters.

SOMEONE REALLY IS STEALING THE TAXPAYERS' MONEY

"Yes," affirmed the auditor, "you are correct. An employee has been, is, or will be stealing from you."

This conversation took place thirty days after the following press release had been issued:

> On Monday, February 13, the City Manager notified the council that city staff had uncovered an alleged embezzlement by an employee in the city's finance department. The City Manager praised city staff and the financial controls in place for bringing the matter to light. According to the manager, the city has a competent staff and good financial controls in place. That is why it was able to uncover this theft. Financial controls serve as a deterrent and ensure that wrongdoers will be caught.

> The alleged embezzlement is believed to approximate twenty thousand dollars and was carried out by altering revenue receipts. The city's outside auditing firm has been brought in to review city records. The firm will be issuing an independent report later this month.

The city expects to recover all of the funds, either from the alleged embezzler or from the insurance company that provides bonding coverage for all employees.

Been There and Seen It

Over the past forty years, I have worked in several local governments with reputations for good government and outstanding financial management. Yet, in each government, at one time or another, an employee has stolen taxpayer money.

In my third management position, the employee taking the money was the finance director himself, who had been an employee of the city for fifteen years. He embezzled more than seventy thousand dollars. Because he had established many of the financial safeguards himself, he thought he could beat the system, and he nearly did, except for a persistent auditor who followed up on a minor discrepancy. The finance director was caught.

At the time when I started employment in my fourth city, a scandal was breaking in the municipal court, where clerks had been accepting payoffs for fixing tickets.

Four years later in the same city, another scandal was uncovered involving the same municipal court, where clerks again were taking payoffs for fixing tickets.

In my fifth city, customers had suspicions about the cash management activities of the acting director of an enterprise fund, a golf course. Sure enough, as soon as a new director was hired, revenues went up.

Food for Thought

I have gained insights from these experiences. In most instances, the embezzler is the average working person, just like you or me.

Embezzlers are well liked, ambitious, have earned people's trust, and generally have no previous criminal record. They have these personality traits that help place them in positions of trust with the opportunity to break the law.

Employees who are involved in these actions do not always view them as crimes. They rationalize their behavior by believing this is a dishonest world, and they are just getting their fair share; or they are getting even for not getting a raise or promotion.

Some consider embezzlement to be borrowing because they tell themselves they intend to repay the money. They do not view it as a personal act against someone or something, as a robbery is, but rather as an inconsequential act that has no effect on the government's deep pockets.

The first factor that leads an employee to steal is motivation. Motivation takes the form of need or greed, whether perceived or real. Often, this motivation is a personal and private financial problem arising out of such causes as a divorce, living beyond one's means, business failure, or a tragic medical problem.

Motivation cannot be controlled. It exists without our influence as managers.

The second factor leading to embezzlement is opportunity. Usually, the embezzler is in a position of trust, with no one checking them closely or monitoring their activities. They see an opportunity in which it is easy and safe to steal, the risk of getting caught is low, and it seems worth the chance. They also may perceive the punishment as minimal if they are caught.

Opportunity can be controlled.

Embezzlement is an insidious crime. A manager can never know when to suspect it, how it will be done, who has done it, or how much money was lost.

Many managers already have been the victims of embezzlement and do not know that it has happened. Most managers will have this experience in their careers.

If you watch your daily newspaper carefully, you will routinely see an article on someone stealing from the employer. But if there are all these embezzlements and stealing taking place, why aren't there even more stories in the newspaper? Most embezzlements don't make the paper.

Think about why that is, if it's so frequent.

It's bad publicity.

Lesson: If you are a City Manager, find a way conduct internal audits. Pick random activities. The message is important to the public and the employees. It will protect you when the inevitable is uncovered.

MISCELLANEOUS

In one city I served in, President Clinton, Vice President Gore, several cabinet members, and Jesse Jackson visited our local high school to announce a national youth support program.

I spent literally a half day at the school with the president and his entourage. History will properly judge President Clinton. However, I need to note that he projects more charisma than anyone I have ever seen or met.

I walked into the challenge of my career as the budget director. My predecessor had been fired after only six weeks on the job. She had been set up by the staff. One of the alleged conspirators was a key person on my staff. In addition, the budget crisis was so serious that three hundred employee jobs were on the line.

I hung on by my fingernails for eighteen months. Then, *our* organizational strategies and hard work began to pay off.

When I left, after three and a half years, there had been only four layoffs, which were unavoidable.

I was touched that as I moved to my new job, the City Manager publicly gave me a special monetary award recognizing my contribution. (I wouldn't have done it.)

I served in a community near Washington, DC, where an unsuccessful candidate for the city council had a full-time job with the CIA. He prepared the president's top secret daily briefing, summarizing world happenings.

I always thought he had an interesting job. I chatted with him about his ambitions to be a part-time elected councilman. He already had one of the most interesting jobs in the country! Turns out, a job is still a job, and he was looking for more challenge. Food for thought!

Weather forecasts predicted the hurricane would hit the Gulf Coast in two days, with a wind speed so great that the instruments in the Gulf of Mexico could not record it.

City ordinances required all city employees to remain in the city during a period of emergency. Leaving the city resulted in automatic dismissal.

We had an eighteen-month-old daughter at the time. My wife was also three months pregnant with our second child.

We were living in a condo on the water. The situation was grave. The water level slowly rose and overflowed into the lower garage area. Preparations were made to evacuate. Estimates warned that the city could be flattened.

While I stayed, I managed to get my wife on the very last plane before they closed the airport. She went to Washington, DC, to stay with her mother. I went further inland in the city and stayed with considerate staff.

The powerful, whirling hurricane in the Gulf of Mexico suddenly swung westward. It hit an unpopulated area of Mexico. Most of the force of the storm dissipated. Only a major rainstorm hit the city. We all breathed a sigh of relief and welcomed the sunshine.

AND THE WALL CAME TUMBLING DOWN

In the 1980s, as a young pup, I had the good fortune to be selected by the International City Management Association and the Council on International Urban Liaison for a six-week exchange program with West Germany. With four ICMA colleagues, we visited twenty-one cities in forty-two days, including East Germany and East Berlin. This was before the Berlin Wall came tumbling down.

I had been unable to talk about this for five years, because I would become too emotional.

At Checkpoint Charlie in West Berlin, I came upon a woman demonstrator. Having just spent time in the Communist East, and thoroughly disgusted with what I had experienced, I was furious and wanted to tell her to take her placards and jump over to the other side of THE WALL.

To my shock, she was pleading for help. The pictures on the placards she was demonstrating with were of her children. The children had been taken by the East Germans when she and her husband had been released from prison and fled west. Their "crime" had been trying to escape to the West. The children were put up for adoption by the communists.

She stood in the cold and rain every day for three months in that high profile location, begging for someone's help. You had to be there to experience her hopeless despair.

I was overwhelmed with rage and helpless frustration. I swallowed hard and blinked rapidly. My eyes were ready to leak, not from the rainy day.

Finally, city management training kicked in, and I decided to take a "management" approach to the problem. Long story short: I sent a letter recommending action back to my mayor, whom I knew I could count on.

A colonel at the Pentagon at the time, we had given the mayor the secret moniker of "Bomb 'em John," reflecting his strong anti-Soviet Empire views. The mayor immediately forwarded my letter to our senator, who contacted the US liaison to East Germany (no ambassador, because no recognition).

Thank you, John.

The children were released.

Lesson: Sometimes you possess more resources than you think.

"KIDS WITH GUNS"

I stood ten feet inside West Germany, at the edge of the weeds and woods. In the thick foliage, twenty steps away, two seventeen-year-old East German soldiers held automatic weapons.

Each communist soldier was trained to shoot his comrade if he tried to escape to the West by running over to our side, in the open field.

We could see the sun glinting off the rifle barrels of other East German soldiers hidden further back in the trees. Their weapons were deployed on their seventeen-year-old comrades as an escape deterrent, in case both made a run for it together.

When a member of our delegation raised his camera to take pictures of the soldiers, they glared and turned their backs. Do you know what it is like to take a picture of a teenager armed with a Kalashnikov, when he doesn't want you taking his picture?

Our delegation, totaling eleven, remained alone and obviously unarmed. Fifteen minutes after we arrived, a US Army jeep came flying over the hill with a real live uniformed lieutenant and sergeant. It felt like a John Wayne movie, the American cavalry coming to our rescue.

Chatting with our "rescuers," we discovered that while the US soldiers were armed, there were no bullets in their guns: orders so that no American would precipitate *an incident*. They would need to load their weapons before they could shoot. The East German kids were armed to the teeth and ready to shoot.

Lesson: Kids shouldn't have automatic weapons, fully loaded.

Don't Mess
With Commies

I strolled through the quaint communist East German town of Eisenach in the 1980s, as part of a US ICMA delegation, alone with my German partner. My adrenaline high telegraphed that we were obviously being followed by a secret policeman wearing the stereotypical black trench coat topped off with a grey Humphrey-Bogart-private-eye fedora.

At least he was color coordinated.

We turned hard right, down the alley.

He followed.

Thinking to discourage him, I quickly turned in the alley and took his picture with my flash camera. I thought he blinked and frowned. We walked on.

He was no longer behind us.

Good.

Message sent.

Minutes later, we turned into a bookstore to browse. I sensed a presence behind me. It was the hat wearer, in a non-hat era, with his secret-police coat standing right behind me, a sardonic half smile pasted on his face. He looked pretty official to me.

My heart dropped. I was scared. We left the shop immediately. As I glanced back in the store window, I observed the undercover agent questioning the shop owner.

Message sent.

Lesson: Don't mess with commies, especially when they wear trench coats and fedoras.

The Bridge At Remagen

During the last week of our six-week US/ICMA program exchange, our West German officials took us on a trip outside Bonn but wouldn't say where we were going.

It turned out that it was a surprise visit for me to the Bridge at Remagen. They had remembered me telling them that my uncle had been the seventh US soldier across that bridge in World War II, when the Germans failed to blow it up. (Remember the movie?)

My uncle had been shot up later that day, after crossing the bridge. He endured multiple knee operations, spent fourteen months in recovery, and a lifetime of fighting pain with alcohol.

Their gesture of taking me to the site touched me.

The gesture was very German.

Bringing Democracy To Eastern Europe

In the 1990s, I was selected for an ICMA delegation attending a conference in Krakow, Poland, to work with ninety Eastern European officials on municipal finance and budget issues.

I was scheduled to make a short presentation on municipal budgeting and then to serve as a facilitator for the Romanian delegation.

It sounded to me like a light-work recipe for European sight-seeing. I prepared to quickly overview the joys and mysteries of municipal budgeting.

Instead, the Romanian delegation wanted to redefine the entire power relationship between local government and the previously ruthless communist central government, run by the dictator Ceausescu and his wife.

The delegation ignored the conference and caucused continuously, seeking occasional comment and advice from me. I had morphed from Budget Guru to National Political Advisor.

The delegation caucused until 3:00 AM.

The next day, the Romanian delegation issued the Krakow Manifesto to the conference. The manifesto sounded like a Balkans version of the Declaration of Independence! Heady stuff! The delegation formally adopted this political statement to diplomatically start a process of reform in Romania. As a result, significant International City Management Association (ICMA) follow-up in Romania took place after the conference, including a special symposium sponsored by the United Nations.

As for the Eastern European sightseeing later in the week: well, that took us to Auschwitz and Birkenau, a two-hour drive from Krakow, in the remote Polish countryside. It vividly brought home all of the Leon Uris novels I had read over the years.

Three details regarding the extermination camps:

First, the German nation was responsible for these horrors. Adolf Hitler had been elected with 43% of the German vote, the same percentage as Bill Clinton in 1992. The Allies downplayed that fact after World War II. We needed the Germans after the war to confront the expansionistic Russians.

Second, when the tour group went into the basement cells where executions took place around the clock, I could *feel evil* and had to leave. It was not my imagination because I'm not built that way.

Thirdly, the large room stacked from floor to ceiling with baby shoes of the original victims made a special statement.

Even though I am half German by ancestry I will not forgive Germany.

3-3-1

In the morning while shaving, I tallied council votes for the millionth time, from every conceivable angle. There had been two council elections since I arrived, with a sea change in council philosophy. The council had morphed from "let's move the community forward quickly," to "how can we maintain and take care of our buddies?"

Yep. It was still four to three in my favor, with the mayor opposed to me. The mayor could only vote if there was a tie. Well, there was no tie. My four votes were solid. The only way the mayor could vote would be if there was an agenda item to dismiss me, and one of my four votes was sick or, or, wait—out of town!

I knew none of the four would vote against me in a public meeting, but could someone be persuaded to be out of town? I redoubled my search efforts for a new job.

Months later, I announced my new City Manager position to the council. As I was leaving, I had lunch with a young council-man supporter. I had always enjoyed and admired his pleasant, competent professionalism and intelligence. The lunch confirmed my previous fear about the possible 4-3-1 math manipulation.

He shared he had been fired from his job several years ago because he ran for the city council, after he was told that it wasn't his turn and he should withdraw from the political race. He ran, almost won, and the good old boys saw that he lost his job.

He remembered.

He liked me and the job I was doing. It was clear that there was no way he would vote to fire me. He revealed to me that the mayor had approached him weeks earlier. Knowing his support for me, the mayor had suggested that all he had to do was to be out of town when my performance review came up.

Lesson: In this business, always have an updated resume.

Lesson: Find ways to secure intelligence on what is really going on. I have not done well at the intelligence gathering.

JAPANESE PROTEST

In the 1990s, I participated in an official US ICMA delegation to Japan. During the visit, Japanese officials briefed us on current issues and presented us with formal studies.

In reading their reports, I discovered that the fertility rate had dropped to 1.53 per couple. I read how the Japanese women were marrying later in life, or not at all.

It was a massive, unspoken, feminine social protest against the chauvinistic strains in Japanese society. These statistics meant that the Japanese nation would disappear in several generations. But, no one talked about this.

At the final briefing as I made my summary observations and we ended our visit, I pointed this out to our Japanese host officials from their own data sources.

The Japanese officials smiled politely.

MONKEY BUSINESS

Doing preparatory newspaper reading for my next City Manager assignment, I came upon the story of The Chimp: a colorful, bizarre story.

As a child-sized, four-year-old chimp in 1970, he attended his adopted human parents' wedding as the best man. He was also an "honorary citizen of the city."

The Chimp had been rescued, several years before the wedding, as a small, orphaned primate in Africa and brought back to the neighborhood. That was thirty years earlier. He was now five foot one, two hundred pounds of furry muscle, packing the upper body strength of four grown men.

Months after I arrived as City Manager, The Chimp escaped from his raised backyard cage behind the house, terrorized a neighbor woman with small kids, bit a police officer, and damaged two police cars.

His owners were masters of manipulating public opinion. Neighbors and friends rallied to the cause of keeping the powerful primate in the neighborhood. The media exploited the news presentation as a "human interest" story and "keeping the family together."

I knew this was an issue I did not want to get enmeshed in. I had heard of similar controversies in other communities where it was a total no-win situation. It would consume enormous time, put the council in a difficult public position, and probably not be resolved.

Instead, I decided that we would bide our time and wait for the right opportunity.

It came one year later, at the cost of a woman's fingertip that the large chimp bit off when she fed him some sweets. So twisted was this episode that the victim would not cooperate with police for fear that her testimony would be used to remove the primate from the tightly packed neighborhood.

There was media attention all the way to western Australia. My assistant's mother sent her a copy of the news article from Down Under, back home.

Two days later, without notice, county animal control and city police moved in to remove the hulking two-hundred-pound animal from the community.

The total casualty rate now included a severely bitten police officer at a taxpayer cost of $250,000, plus the officer's pain and suffering; two damaged police cars; and a woman with her fingertip bitten off.

Still, staunch remnants of support for The Chimp remained from the larger community. News stories portrayed the chimp from their old file photos as the cuddly three year old in his cute tuxedo suit. There were few photos of *THE HULK*.

Immediate neighbors felt differently. The animal had taken them hostage with his intimidating behavior, noise, and his smell. Occasionally, he would throw his feces around.

Enter stage left, a nationally known, high profile media attorney, the newly hired advocate for the chimp. In her trademark red suit, the attractive barrister played the media like a skilled concert violinist.

The negative impacts on the lives and safety of the neighbors by this primate never received any coverage. Late night bellowing, barnyard smells, and mammal masturbation in full view weren't as interesting for the media to report as was the story of the government trying to break up a nontraditional family.

Additional collateral damage included a change in the council majority after the election, in which the primate had become an issue. Pro-chimp sentiment carried the day.

With incredible good fortune, I was able to announce my acceptance of a City Manager job in another city, one day after the election.

Lesson: If the city has monkey business, keep your resume updated.

[A tragic footnote: several years later, after The Chimp had been moved to a wildlife preserve, his "parents" went to see him, as they often did. During their visit, two other large chimps roamed on the loose and quickly started toward the wife, biting her left thumb off. The husband positioned himself to protect her from further attack. Turning on him, they mauled him mercilessly, biting off fingers, his nose, his lips and his genitals.]

Everyone's "Rights"

Today, as a public official, you can be on the receiving end of charges alleging discrimination based on race, gender, religion, sexual preference, disability, age, retaliation, sexual harassment, or creating a hostile workplace. Sometimes, these legal protections provide unfair cover for incompetence or worse. This potential for charges, sometimes spurious, always gives one pause before going forward with disciplinary actions or termination.

Having grown up during the civil rights revolution, I have understood and supported the need for change to protect against discrimination.

I have been unfairly subjected to two civil rights actions: One was by a White police officer who complained about my hiring a Black officer. The Black officer scored higher on our assessment matrix. The unsuccessful White officer candidate was the personal friend of a White police lieutenant on our force.

The second action involved a ten-million-dollar civil rights lawsuit filed against me by the White owner of a recycling center in a large city where I was the City Manager. It turned out that the enterprise displayed more of the characteristics of an unlawful dump, approximately five acres in size and three stories high. It caught on fire and burned for twenty-eight days. To put the fire out, it took state and federal teams, as well as our own fire department, at a total cost of six million dollars.

Damage to the community's air and environment was significant. I did everything I could to shut the owner down, within the law, and hold him accountable for the harm he caused. We believed lives may have been lost because of the air pollution.

Several years later, he sued unsuccessfully. Fortunately, at the time of the burning dump incident, when I was hell-bent on closing his business immediately, I had reluctantly followed the advice of our city attorney to revoke the owner's permit through the appropriate process, meticulously.

Good advice.

Lesson: Sorry to sound like an old curmudgeon, but sometimes good intentions (and good laws) get perverted. Then, we wonder why government is so slow and cautious.

Ego Check

The overhaul of the General Plan, the growth roadmap for the city's future, was big news. Divisive politics, big developer money, smart growth ideology, inner-city land economics, racial demographics—all were on the table to be put in the political cooking pot for boiling. Quite a recipe for either a delicious stew or a yucky, tasteless broth.

After the first acrimonious debate by the city council, the mayor and I stepped out into the long, gray-carpeted hallway next to the city council chamber, trailed by reporters and cameramen.

In the bullring circle of bright camera lights, the charismatic, high-profile mayor fielded the questions like the pro, the trained actor, he was. In front of the camera, he made magic. He provided responsive, folksy but erudite answers showing how these seemingly arcane legislative planning changes could shape the positive, new future of the city.

After ten minutes of the media game, the reporters started to repeat themselves and to drift away from the immediate, important topic.

The mayor announced, "You all know our City Manager here. He's well versed in these issues and can answer your additional questions. I need to be at another meeting. Thank you very much."

The mayor stepped away from the inquiring, pushy horde, leaving me alone in the white circle of light.

Click. Click. Click. Click.

All the cameras turned off.

I stood there, waiting for follow-up questions, a little nervous but prepared for Q and A on the proposed new General Plan.

Chatting among themselves, youngish reporters and their appendage-like camera men ambled away down the hall.

I had been taught in the profession, and believed, the City Manager should be behind the scenes, low profile. The media did too. But...

SOLUTION TO THE PROBLEM OF FREQUENT CHANGES OF EMPLOYERS

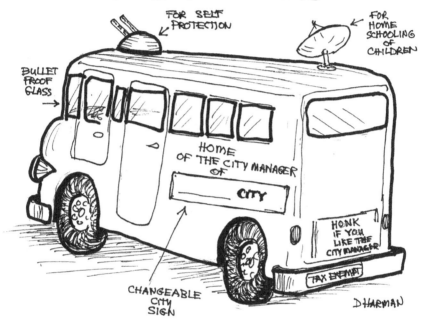

DIDN'T GET
THE JOB (WHEW!)

Some of the best things that ever happened to me in city management were jobs that I interviewed for and didn't get. How about this:

Being interviewed by a panel in a Texas community, one panel member is the president of the local NAACP, another panel member's brother is reported to be the secret leader of the local KKK. And then, the panel asks me for my views on affirmative action!

I told them.

Being interviewed by the city council in Colorado, I discovered one of the council leaders was a strict libertarian — believing in little or no government! Huh?

What are you doing on the city council?

I interviewed for the City Manager job in the LA area where the community was 90 percent Hispanic, and the council was all Hispanic.

That was fine with me because my wife and kids are Hispanic, and I prefer Hispanic people. No patronizing attitude on my part—just a personal, joyful embrace of that culture.

The council was politically divided—unfortunately, a common situation. Didn't get the nod.

One year later, I visually stumbled across the Internet video of the mayor publicly announcing his personal bankruptcy, his business bankruptcy, and his six-month separation from his wife, and he then acknowledged that he was having an affair with one of the council women.

Grim as that picture was, it got worse. The mayor's wife was in the audience, irate, and had to be escorted from the council chamber by the police, and all on public video.

You have to love the drama of this business!

As a young man, I was interviewed for an Assistant City Manager position across the country in Colorado. The visit went on for three days. I had lunch with the City Manager, breakfast with the department heads, and so on.

Exhibiting my usual impatience, I asked, "When is the interview?"

The City Manager responded, "What do you think we've been doing?"

Didn't get the job.

The recruiter called to say that I was scheduled for an interview with the City Manager of the large city, population one million. It was for the top Assistant City Manager position, with a likelihood to succeed the City Manager when he planned to retire in three years.

The city was a weather paradise, with a strong city management tradition. But, I had reservations. Would I just get lost in the shuffle? Did I really want the frantic pace? I consulted a close colleague who had been an assistant there years earlier.

His observations about the government: There were ten councilmen, each with six full-time aides. Worse, each aide acted like he or she was the council member.

The City Manager had more than sixty people telling him what to do.

In addition, according to the former assistant, working there was like having to cross the rocks in a deep, running stream of water. The problem was, some of the rocks were really eggshells, and you didn't know which was which until you stepped on them.

I contacted the recruiter and said I decided to stay where I was.

Three years later, as the City Manager retired, the city was engulfed in complete political turmoil and pension scandals. It triggered federal investigations that are still ongoing.

I interviewed with the mayor for the city administrator position. I made my case strongly and impressed the council in my interview with them. I didn't get the job.

I found out several years later that the mayor was indicted on federal charges, and a councilwoman was suspected of murdering her husband. Allegedly, the police chief had been having an affair with the councilwoman. He was believed to have covered up critical evidence immediately before police investigators responded to the scene of the reported suicide.

And I thought it was a great little town!

I interviewed for budget director of a county of two million people. They wanted me for the job. I would have been working on the third floor of an old building that had been a schoolbook storage building back in the early 1960s.

It had since been converted to county administrative offices. Three floors up, on the sixth floor, Lee Harvey Oswald fired his rifle from this building in 1963 and killed President Kennedy.

The racial politics was bitter, and it was clear I would be suspect, having been declared permanently White.

Been there, done that, got the T-shirt.

Through the large window of the conference room, where the interview was being held, you could see the White House, the Capitol, and the Washington Monument. It was designed to impress. It succeeded.

This was the second interview, down to three finalists. One of the elected board members complimented me on my extraordinary career record of equal opportunity.

He then noted that his community had a very significant gay and lesbian population. (From my research, I knew he had been president of the local gay/lesbian alliance.)

He understood my position of acceptance and tolerance, but he felt we needed to go beyond that and move to, as he put it, "celebration" of the differences. He wanted to know if I could "lead the parade." There was a subtle but pushy, pointed undertone to the question.

My response was simple and to the point. I said, "No." This was a new contemporary issue for me at that time, with lots of nuances.

I heard later that both his colleagues and the executive recruiter felt the question was inappropriate. I wished I had been less direct and had elaborated more in my response. The position was offered to one of the other three finalists, who turned it down. He told me why, years later: "They were crazy!"

As a footnote, at a later time, I faced a kindred decision. I was in a brutally tough political environment, poised to make a key executive hire. The personnel director advised me, even though it was unrelated to the job, that the proposed hire was most probably gay. I hesitated. I envisioned destructive, gossipy politics being used against the candidate in order to attack me. It would be a slow, political unwind, not a confrontation over merit hiring principles.

I had a quick fifteen-second conversation with myself. The candidate brought great credentials to the table. Did I really believe in merit hiring: disregarding religion, race, marital status, sexual preference? I said I did. I practiced this my entire career.

It was a short conversation. I completed the hire.

The new executive was well received and popular with everyone, including the council.

I was one of the unsuccessful finalists for the high-quality, medium-sized community out West that possessed a strong commitment to the environment.

Years earlier, the City Manager finalist there had inquired about a city car or a car allowance. The council said they'd provide a bicycle. The smile left his face when all of sudden, he understood they weren't kidding. He withdrew from consideration.

Several years later I talked to the successful candidate for the City Manager position. He was not happy there.

Got the call from a nationally known City Manager who was acting as one of several interim assistant city administrative officers for a high-profile city.

They were putting a professional, hard-running team in place. They were each charged with going out and recruiting their respective successors. The call was a professional fantasy for me: having sufficient credentials that someone would actually call me, unsolicited, about an important job.

I asked for twenty-four hours to consider it. Even though I was in the market, I did not believe I was a match for the extraordinary challenges, many of which I felt were out of the control of any administration. I think I was right, because the city's chief administrative officer left eighteen months later.

It had been fun to get the call, though, because the caller and I had competed against each other for two attractive city positions in the past. Neither of us got them.

The phone call came through from the high-profile county manager, to me, the young Assistant City Manager working in a quality, comfortable suburb.

I had been an intern for him years ago. He was now the county manager for one of the largest jurisdictions in the Southern part of the country, and he needed a loyal assistant.

Being originally from the Midwest, and having always despised the cold winters there, this was a dream come true. I could work in vacationland! I wrestled with the decision, called him back, thanked him, and turned him down with some reason or another.

The truth was that I was intimidated by the job challenge, even though it would have been extraordinarily interesting. I was afraid to step out.

I took a vacation day, slipped out of town, and flew across the country for the interview. I made air stops in two cities, trying to make the 4:30 PM interview. It was close. The airport taxi pulled up to city hall at 4:20. I was beat.

City officials asked me if I needed anything. I asked for a bathroom break and a cup of coffee, pulled myself together, and pasted on a friendly smile.

The interview went amazingly well. I usually do a good interview when I am tired and therefore tell it like it is, with a little discretion. The interview lasted ninety minutes. The executive recruiter said he'd call me later at the hotel.

The recruiter called an hour later. He said the council had just voted publicly to hire me. He and the mayor wanted to meet at the hotel and work out a contract that evening.

Great!

Three weeks earlier I had withdrawn from this same competition because it was right before the municipal election in my home town. I feared that if my interest became public, it could negatively impact the election. The election went to hell, anyhow, so I was back.

At the hotel meeting, we went down a checklist of items. The recruiter facilitated agreement on one provision after another. We were moving right along.

Then, the phone rang. It was the vice mayor, who was a close political friend of the mayor's. The mayor reported back from the phone call that the vice mayor and one other councilman thought they were moving too fast. There was an undercurrent, an insinuated statement.

I wasn't that crazy about the city, so I said directly to the recruiter, "Should I go back tomorrow or stay another day?" The look in his eyes matched his reply: "Go back home, and I will call you."

Two days later back at work, my secretary handed me a phone message. It was from a reporter in the town where I had interviewed. The reporter wanted to know why I had withdrawn my candidacy. Of course, this was a surprise to my secretary, as well as me.

I called the recruiter to see if I had withdrawn my candidacy. He said yes, in order to protect me politically back home.

A year later, at the annual International City Management Association conference, I talked to the new City Manager they had hired. Apparently, the mayor and a couple of councilmen had been playing "stall ball" with the City Manager selection process. They had pulled the same delay stunt on a candidate before me and after me. They wanted to drag it out until the November election when they felt they could accomplish a clean sweep on the council. Then, they could get someone to carry their water for them.

The hired City Manager had told them what his terms were and that they had forty-eight hours to decide. He was an experienced, principled manager backed up by enough years in the state pension system to retire at any time. I knew he would do a good job for that community.

He did.

"We Need You"

City Managers want to be loved too, like everyone else. I have always felt weak at the knees whenever an elected official has said, "We need you!"

I called the mayor on Monday, after the Saturday interview, to withdraw from the City Manager recruitment. After all, the council furiously argued for ten minutes in my interview over the role of developing a master plan for the community.

I had listened attentively, and then they asked me for my views. I correctly sensed it was a divided council and community and gave them my views on quality, planned development.

In my Monday phone call, the mayor had then pushed all the right buttons. He gushed that I was energetic, proactive, visionary, full of good ideas—just what the community needed. He said he was still suffering from the recent death of his brother, and his voice choked up. He personally needed me there to move the community forward. Would I come back for a second visit?

I did.

I took the job.

The mayor did not run for reelection three months later. I left after eighteen months.

I had flown across country for the interview. I didn't know the community that well, but the climate was great and so were the pay and benefits. I was serious about the position.

The previous City Manager had taken the job and attended the council meeting with his relatives, where he was introduced to the community.

After seeing the adversarial council dynamics in action that evening, he resigned the next day and stayed in his old job. The mayor of the spurned city read about it in the newspaper the next morning. He had not been called yet.

In my subsequent interview, weeks later, the councilwoman spoke plaintively, "We need a good City Manager. We need someone like you. If we offer you the position, will you take it?"

I responded, "Yes."

After the interview, the city attorney persuaded me to call the previous City Manager of that city so that I was sure of what I was getting into. That struck me as an unusual recruiting strategy. My predecessor wasn't home.

I took the job. It was a tough assignment.

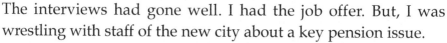

The interviews had gone well. I had the job offer. But, I was wrestling with staff of the new city about a key pension issue.

Finally, the strongly religious mayor called and said, "You will need to decide what you want to do on the pension issue. But, I know in my heart you belong here with us. I feel very strongly that the Lord wants you here. You are the right guy for this city."

Having a strongly religious background myself, there was no way I could refuse the mayor and the Lord.

I got out of bed that morning with a sense of dread. I faced rounds of interviews for a high-profile City Manager position.

While shaving, I did a mental self-examination and said, "You can keep that negative attitude and go nowhere, or you can look at this as an opportunity to meet your newest best friends."

I chose the best friends approach and actually enjoyed the interviews. In the ten-member community panel interview, one panelist asked me if I was bilingual (English/Spanish).

I assumed she was, so I took a risk.

I responded, "Yo hablo Español en mi corazon, but I am not bilingual." (I speak Spanish in my heart, but I am not bilingual.) I elaborated that my wife and children are Hispanic. After the interview, I asked her if my response was within bounds. She responded it was fine.

After the third panel interview, one of the panelists escorted me out into the hallway and said quietly, "Are you sure you want to come here? City Managers only last two to three years here." That struck me as an unorthodox recruiting technique.

I told him I was aware of the tough political reputation and was ready.

I lasted four years.

Well, regarding the best friends psychology that I used on myself, when the executive recruiter had called, she said, "They loved you."

I responded, "That's great. When's the next interview?"

She responded, "There isn't any. You've got the job."

So, lesson learned: when you put out the positive vibe, you get it back.

THE CARDBOARD BOX

Just chatting with the mayor's aide…

I worked hard to get along with him. I admired his intelligence and strong commitment to improving the city. But, I couldn't stand his negative, intimidating approach to people and problems. I always kept my feelings in check, because he was the "Mayor's Man." I was jealous of that. As City Manager that should have been my role.

From the time of the initial job interview, I pegged him as a political hack. That wasn't fair, because he was exceptionally skilled, although a difficult personality and not Mr. Warmth. He would occasionally describe himself as the mayor's rear end. Even though he accepted his role as the bad cop in a good cop/bad cop strategy, it occasionally tugged him down, understandably. We all want a little love sometimes, don't we?

The aide and I worked together business-like for three years, like two porcupines making love. We stayed out of each other's way and played in our own sandboxes as much as possible.

Then, when the mayor became more active on the state and national scene, the aide began stepping in more and more in city hall matters. It felt like I was fighting a two-front war, taking on Herculean city management issues and having to politically watch my back so that I wasn't getting tackled by my own backfield. There seemed to be more and more of that backfield tackling going on. That was disheartening in light of the large number of touchdowns the team had scored.

This aide was interfering daily, although I'm sure he perceived it as assisting or performing a needed liaison role.

Running for the goal line started to feel like wading through quicksand.

So, in this conversation between me and the aide, we were chatting about various organizational dynamics and politics and the differences between those dynamics in the public sector and the private sector, where he had spent much of his career.

He noted how they played hardball in the private sector, especially when they let people go. With what seemed like an unusually poignant look at the time, he said, "You're carrying your cardboard box with you out to the car, and you don't even know what happened."

That conversation stayed with me.

Three weeks later, I was carrying my cardboard boxes, with my kids' help, out to the car. I deliberately had them assist me so they could see their very powerful, high-profile City Manager father leave with quiet dignity, holding in check the anger and hurt. It didn't mean anything to my children then, but it would as they got older.

A week after leaving city hall, I returned to pick up my generous separation check, and I ran into the aide. He told me that when he had heard about my meeting with the mayor and my resignation, he had cried. My problem was, I believed him.

Go figure.

A footnote: two years after this, the mayoral aide ended up resigning in disgrace over harassment allegations. I initially experienced smug feelings of vindication, but, surprising to me, more sadness that he had been consumed by the organization's historical culture of eating its young. He had worked so hard for the mayor and the city.

Later, I shared those reactions with several of his still-remaining colleagues. I was shocked. There was no sympathy at all.

Today, I view him as a casualty of a tough local government dynamic, prevalent in many places, where you become a high-profile target when you make needed change. Despite his shortcomings, he fought hard to make a difference in that community. Being financially well off, he did not need the job.

How Do You Mend
A Broken Heart?

I don't know about other City Managers, but I've always had the problem of falling in love with the cities I serve. Maybe it's because I really get charged up about improving the community I serve — and, love is blind. I want my community to be the best in the world. If I'm not careful, I can be messianic about it, and that leads to political problems. We all know what happens to messiahs.

Being in love with your community can be a real problem when it is time to move on.

Early in my career, I stumbled into a great situation. It was a wonderful community, in a wonderful location; my job commute was five minutes, I had a super boss, and as an Assistant City Manager I made as much money as many small town City Managers.

I was comfortable. It took a cannon to propel me out of there.

That cannon arrived on the scene when the City Manager I worked for left, and I applied for the job.

I came in second place for the City Manager job. The new City Manager visited before starting the job and requested that I stay on and help him. I was pleased and relieved to do so.

Six weeks later, he advised that he would be doing a reorganization, and there wouldn't be a position for me. That was one of the few nights in my life that I did not sleep. I never did get closure on the real reason for the musical chairs; maybe it was just what he told me: "You understand that a CEO needs to be able to select his own people around him."

I still have a piece of my heart, and relatives, in that community.

I needed to move organizationally. I had stayed too long in my happy cocoon. I was too complacent, although I explored ways to stay energized.

Like a jilted lover, I swore to never fall in love with a city again. But, life goes on with amazing twists and turns. I've worked in some wonderful places, but none exactly like that city.

And, here's a real irony about the cannon that propelled me out. I respected the credentials and experience he brought. He was very smart, a veteran CEO. But there was a sense of ruthless efficiency about him. I didn't think he fully appreciated our culture, our mores, our little nuances in doing things, our need to take a little more time for change because we thought we were already pretty good. He was impatient: seemed to know everything and had already been there, done that and was waving the T-shirt.

I took offense at our conversations where I was not able to finish my comments before he interjected with proposed solutions, usually very good ones I hadn't thought of. My feelings were hurt because as I mentally huddled with myself, I admitted his instincts were accurate and his recommendations sound.

Several City Manager positions later, as I reflected back on this experience with a subordinate, I shared this intimate story to communicate to the subordinate that maybe the subordinate was like me back then, too comfortable.

In the same conversation, engaging in some verbal self-reflection, I wondered if I had now become that same cannon. Because at this point, I too was always in a hurry, really did know a lot, and wanted and needed change quickly.

REFLECTIONS ON
PERFECTION

Have you ever read the job ads for City Manager positions? The civilian translation of many of them is "able to leap tall buildings in a single bound;" "faster than a speeding bullet."

You get the idea.

Those ads used to intimidate me. I couldn't do all of those things and be everything to everyone.

Over the years, I gradually became less intimidated as I sent out a résumé or two and actually interviewed, and, in some cases, got hired!

As I met more and more City Managers, I noticed they didn't have an *S* engraved on their chests. In fact, they were like me: credentialed, dedicated, and flawed.

So, with a lot of experience behind me, these would be my takeaways:

Yes, the community you come in to serve does expect you to be Superman or Superwoman. However, if you try to get the job done as a one-person show, you will be exposed to deadly kryptonite, sooner, not later.

If there is a dysfunctional council, a structural budget deficit, an intractable racial divide: yep, you are to fix it. The really amazing thing about this profession and my colleagues is that they do fix things.

Because of the high profile and fishbowl impact of our positions, we are held up to constant scrutiny by everyone: elected officials, community, staff, and even family.

It is understandable that these folks might have different agendas and that you may not be able to please everyone. So, you are perceived as: too tough or not tough enough; communicates poorly or talks too much; empowers and challenges staff or too threatening to staff; holds the line against special interests or insensitive to the community's history and needs.

You can expand the list.

The perpetual guillotine of firing hangs menacingly over our heads in this business of public management. Maybe we call it "transition" or "waiting for the next assignment" or "on the beach."

We talk like we acknowledge it, but we're very upset when it happens. We then jeopardize our self-esteem, which can undercut the requirements for the high energy, positive enthusiasm, and other characteristics necessary for the next successful job search.

We know it's a hazard of the business, because it happens frequently. Yet, the fired manager is usually at a disadvantage for a lot of reasons in the job search. It shouldn't be that way; it is not fair. But it's there.

I remember a terrible saying in the profession: "You're not a real City Manager unless you've been fired at least once."

I hate that saying.

The saying is true.

I think the really good City Managers recognize these risks and the contradictions. They find ways to meet them through clarity of purpose, commitment to public service, strong family support, constant self-improvement, and good employment contracts.

CITY MANAGER EVALUATION PROCESS

EVALUATION GEMS

Evaluation time can be difficult and tricky, or it can be pretty good.

Pretty good has sounded like: "We think you are so wonderful that…" and I start to blush. (That only happened once.) Usually it's, "You're doing a good job, and we'd like to adjust your pay by X."

Difficult can take this form: the mayor, opening the evaluation discussion with his assessment, says, "I don't trust you."

Because he and his colleague had tried to sell out the city, literally, several times, I responded in kind: "You don't trust me? I don't trust you any further than I can throw you!" (He and his political sidekick were very, very big guys, physically.)

My simplistic comeback felt great at the moment. It was justified and completely unprofessional. A later reality check with the other council members who were present revealed that they had engaged in mental applause at my heated rebuttal. But, why didn't they weigh in? They were tired of doing battle and were a little intimidated by the terrible two.

An unusual evaluation took place years ago in another city. There had been a dramatic change in council. The new council was very different from the one that hired me. It was evaluation time, and I was waiting after the council meeting for the council to conclude their internal discussion. And I was waiting, and waiting, and waiting.

Maybe this was good. They were obviously taking this seriously and discussing all of my great work and the new ideas and energy I brought to the city.

After two hours of waiting, I concluded this may not be so good.

At the two-and-a-half-hour mark, they brought me in. The council was split on my performance. The mayor was especially critical because he said I had called the council "corrupt." "Corrupt?" I didn't recall ever saying that. He responded by saying that I had, by referring to the council as "contentious."

I and another member of the Council explained the meaning of the word, "contentious," and everyone agreed that the council was contentious. That clarification didn't change the mayor's mind, of course.

You Really Can't
Go Home Again

After years of City Manager assignments all over the country, I was headed back home to the Midwest to serve in a quality, progressive community.

Incongruities began to appear. We were fifteen minutes from one of the largest Black populations in the country. Yet, there was not one Black employee in the city hall building. This was decades after the civil rights marches.

Several months into the job, I was recruiting for my executive secretary's position. I did something different from their usual recruiting practice: I advertised in the newspaper. Because of this "unusual" recruitment technique, two of the three finalists ended up being Black.

One Black finalist had scored third in the state stenographic contest, but she was young and outspoken, and I felt she wouldn't take crap off anybody. I suspected there was some crap out there.

I chose the other Black candidate with two years of college. She was a pleasant, mature woman who was more qualified than the third, who was a White candidate. The White candidate was politically connected, having worked for a local judge. But, she only had a high school education.

Three months into my new secretary's tenure, I began to receive organizational feedback about her mistakes and how they were reflecting on me. I took the comments seriously.

Then I realized that the other secretary in the office, who was new and also very hard working, made mistakes too. But no one seemed to make a big deal out of them, including me. The other secretary was White.

The personnel director visited. He wanted to talk to me about the accountant position they were preparing to fill in the finance department. It was down to two candidates: one was White, with a high school degree; the other was Black, with a college degree in accounting.

The finance director wanted to hire the White candidate. Baffled, I asked why. He said the finance director felt the White candidate "would fit in better."

Those were the words.

I told the personnel director I was so angry I couldn't talk to the finance director and to go hire the Black candidate. If anyone had a problem with that, they could come talk to me.

Later, I reviewed this proposed injustice and potential for litigation with the mayor. He displayed a studied non-reaction. Why?

I was disappointed in his weak response because he prided himself on his civil rights credentials.

I made a point to go visit the new Black accountant after she was hired. She struck me as a very nice person in addition to having the needed credentials for the job.

She was heavyset. Most of the women in the department were svelte.

Then, a key executive position opened up. I recruited and was excited to be narrowing the search to an exceptional Black candidate whom I wanted to hire.

All hell broke loose. The council wanted me to slow down; maybe set up a committee to interview finalists; maybe reexamine if we needed to fill the position, and so on.

I lost that candidate who went on years later to be the City Manager of one of the largest, most progressive cities in the Southwest.

Later, word filtered back to me that I wasn't really a good fit for the organization. I received a confidential phone call from an ex-employee over the weekend that there was a political plan to have the assistant replace me the following year.

Then, I discovered that the personnel director in whom I had confided my frustrations had gone to high school with the council member leading the charge behind the scenes to quietly remove me.

When I saw the personnel director at our church with his lovely wife and three adorable children, I had little love in my heart, even though I was in the Lord's house.

After I moved on, the assistant became the City Manager, and the personnel director became Assistant City Manager. I had been in the way, and I certainly didn't fit in with the traditions of "the club."

I realized the Midwest hadn't changed that much.

I had.

MANAGEMENT IS SO DUMB!

"You guys in management are so dumb that you don't know that when we don't feel like working, we just drive around town in the city trucks!"

This was the chief labor representative speaking at our joint labor/management productivity task force. He became so impassioned that he forgot he was talking to the City Manager. I just mentally filed it.

Since his statement, I've never looked at city trucks driving around town the same way.

WILL I GET ANY SEVERANCE?

"Will I get any severance?" he asked. The embattled department director sat across from me at the blond-wooded conference table. The previous mayor had commended me for keeping this director and others on during the change in mayoral administrations. I told the ex-mayor that I was focused on talent, not politics.

I called the meeting with the director to tell him I was firing him, effective immediately. He had been under criticism in the newspaper for a high-profile project that was off budget and very late. But that wasn't why we were meeting.

He had violated the law in the course of his duties, and it was in the newspaper and grabbing the public's attention. After I also realized he had lied to me about the incident, through omission, I had no alternative.

I liked him. He was exceptionally personable and a great salesman.

Later, I remarked to the mayor how much it hurt to do my job that day. The mayor commented with a nugget of wisdom. "If you couldn't do what you had to do, you'd be the wrong guy for the job. If it didn't bother you to do what you had to do, you'd be the wrong guy for the job." I heard him and felt a little better.

Again, I really liked the guy.

PROMINENT CITIZEN
SELLS OUT

It was evening at the city/chamber of commerce out-of-town conference, with an eclectic group at the bar having a nightcap. The socializers included me as City Manger, the Assistant City Manager, the mayor, the police chief, and the chamber of commerce executive director. We had been joined by a prominent, well-regarded citizen who was also a former council member.

The former council member and I belonged to the same service club back home. I frequently bent his ear, complaining of borderline corruption by two current members of the council, as well as their unconscionable bullying tactics against anyone who disagreed with them.

Midway through our group elbow bending, our prominent and affluent citizen announced he was putting up a seventy-thousand-dollar war chest to defeat the two "bully boys." He had had enough. He wanted to protect the city he loved. We were impressed.

The election came. We really didn't hear much from Prominent Citizen. The election went the wrong way. The long knives came out.

Months later, in my new city as City Manager, I was informed that Prominent Citizen had been a plant all along, keeping the bad guys informed of our moves and conversations on city issues.

What a disappointment.

THEY HAD THEIR CHANCE

One of my best assignments was working for a medium-sized, high-quality community in suburban Washington DC. Being in the metro area presented constant opportunity for new experiences.

I attended a small, ten-couple, Saturday evening party given by friends with an international Hispanic background. Without warning, I stumbled into two dramatic, juxtaposed cocktail conversations that left my head reeling with historic revisionisms.

In the first, I chatted with a vivacious woman in her thirties, hair so blonde it was almost white, the eyes a pure sky blue, all of which highlighted the green sheen of her stylish silk dress, cut slightly above slim knees. I remarked on her slightly accented English. She replied that she was German, from Argentina.

I learned my World War II history at the knee of an expert, my father, who was a D-day-plus-thirty veteran. I maneuvered the chitchat around to "What did your father do in the war"?

I did not anticipate her blood-smeared answer. She casually replied he was in the SS. He moved to Argentina after the war to "avoid all the politics."

Practicing the art of indirection, I referred to the alleged reputation of the SS. She acknowledged the accusatory history but, with a dismissive tone, labeled most of it as propaganda written by the victors. She added that no one really knew what was going on since war time Germany was a closed police state with no information available.

Her husband, a handsomely dark, Hispanic son of Argentina in an expensive tweed sports coat, joined the conversation. He was a well-educated, midlevel staffer with the US State Department. He acknowledged allegations against the SS, as he tossed them with rhetorical skill into a conversational dustbin, noting that both sides committed atrocities during a terrible war.

I mentioned my occasional interaction with an up-and-coming state legislator, a contemporary, in the nearby city where I worked for the local government.

I described him as Cuban and Jewish. "Can you believe how international this Washington region has become?"

In line with our conversation, I also observed that his wife was born in the camps, during the war. I further noted that she had always struck me as wearing a tragic air about her, a dark, sad scarf of despair. It was palpable. Her eyes seemed to be tragic pools. I told them I had made this observation to myself when I first met her, before I knew her European story.

The Argentinian husband commented, with an ever-so-slightly-arrogant undertone, "They had their chance."

Refusing to believe what I thought I was hearing, seeming to be puzzled, I asked him to clarify.

"The Jews; they had their chance to get out of Germany," he said.

Shocked, not wanting to overreact, which could have lead to strong words and some me-on-him-bitch-slapping, I politely wrapped up the conversation and moved on.

(This Argentinian guy works for our State Department? *Who let him in!*)

I knew World War II history well, with my self-selected curriculum of Leon Uris novels, most notably *Exodus*, which left a lasting emotional imprint on me from age fourteen.

In addition, eleven years earlier, I had seriously dated a Jewish girl in graduate school.

My dad fought the Germans and saw the atrocities first hand. Eighty-four prisoners had been held by the Germans in a barn in the German countryside. They burned the barn down as they retreated, shooting anyone trying to escape.

My dad's unit came on the barn and forced the nearby German villagers to bury the bodies. Knowing some German from his college classes, he overheard their whispers: "Our boys didn't do this. The Americans did this and are blaming it on us."

Less than ten minutes later, I had another conversation at the same small party.

I chatted up a friendly, pleasant-looking woman, also in her early thirties. She projected an attractive, low-key, intelligent energy, despite the black glasses and the formless gray wool skirt. Engaging, she spoke with a British accent.

With friendly interest, I inquired about her origins.

She was from Germany, the post-war part that was under British occupation. She learned her English from the Brits.

I pointed out, "I just met another person at this same party, also with a German background."

When she replied, "I know, I met her," there was a slight hesitation in the eyes. I asked about her father and the war. She stunned me: "He was in a concentration camp."

"Was he Jewish?"

"No."

"A political enemy?"

"No. He refused to fight in the war."

"A conscientious objector?" I pursued.

"No, he was just opposed to the war and didn't agree with what was going on."

I had never heard of a civilian, nonpolitical German taking this stance.

I continued, "But how did he even know what was going on? The government controlled all the media with their propaganda and restricted the information!"

She replied, "No, we knew. There was enough information out there about what was going on. My father was opposed, and they arrested him. People generally knew what was going on."

DID I MAKE
A WRONG TURN?

Talking to my twenty-two-year-old champion daughter, I found out that in her sales and marketing position, if she secured the assistant manager promotion she had been working so hard on for the last eighteen months, she'd make more money than I did as City Manager in most of the cities I served. In her company, moving up is based strictly on performance by meeting the numbers. She's also a good team leader and a wonderful person.

I compared the predominantly quantitative evaluation process used in her work with that used in my business. In my line of work, the ultimate evaluation comes from an elected board of five or seven people from the community.

There are other evaluations occurring simultaneously, feeding into the elected officials:

- What do the unions think?
- How does the business community react to him?
- How do the senior staff feel?
- How does that department director or Assistant City Manager who wanted his job feel?
- What is the press coverage?
- How does he compare to his predecessor?

- How do special interests x, y, and z feel, in particular, special interest y, which provided campaign contributions to me?
- How is he perceived by the neighborhood associations?
- How is he received by the minority communities?
- How does he get along with each of us?
- Do we like him?

"ON THE BEACH"
CITY MANAGERS IN TRANSITION

RESCUED FROM
THE BEACH

Over the years, I enjoyed the candid personal stories of success, failure, and luck from veteran local government managers. The perennial fear of being in transition or "on the beach" someday always haunted me.

Well, I sidestepped the ax for thirty-seven years in the business.

Under a hybrid strong-mayor form of government in a large city, I worked for the mayor as City Manager. My job was to embrace his vision of a high-performance city hall and equal opportunity for everyone. I did so with enthusiasm and loyalty for four years.

Five months after a national article appeared celebrating the successes we had realized in our city, the mayor called me into his office. Coming out of that meeting was a mutual agreement that the time was right to make a change, as he was beginning his second term. I was treated fairly, with twelve months of severance and five months' vacation pay.

I told the mayor, sincerely, that I had been dedicated to his city vision before I arrived and would feel the same way after I left. If I could best support his program by stepping aside, and if it was time to do so, then I would, keeping it all on a high plane.

In concluding my meeting with the Mayor, I made three requests: (1) that I would prepare a very supportive letter of resignation, effective immediately (no use in hanging around); (2) that he would honor my contract; and (3) that he would give me a good letter of recommendation.

He replied that I had these things without even having to ask for them. He offered me another position in the city government, but I respectfully and gratefully declined.

This was characteristic of our relationship of mutual respect and friendship. Of course, the change still hurt.

That night, after I told my wife, I called an executive recruiter friend to share my new status.

He said, "Have you looked at your e-mail tonight? I'm inviting you to interview for two cities in the next three weeks!"

One city paid thirty thousand dollars more than I was being paid; the second city paid ninety thousand dollars more.

Two days after my meeting with the mayor, on the official day of my resignation, I had a phone interview at the request of a different search firm about the City Manager opening in a southwest city with a population of one million.

Four days after that, yet another search firm called to see if I might still be interested in a position that I had checked out the previous fall. I said I was very interested.

Over the next two weeks, I sent out résumés, filled out supplemental questionnaires, and had a number of phone interviews.

Three weeks after my resignation, I officially accepted a new City Manager position with a smaller community, but one not too far away from where I was living. It came with a 25 percent pay increase and substantial, needed housing loan assistance.

Most important for me, I had fallen in love with the city council in the interview. I hadn't planned on it, wasn't in the mood for it, and didn't expect it; but it happened, and I was energized.

At the time I accepted the new job, seven cities were in various stages of discussion with me about city management positions, which included two challenging Assistant City Manager positions.

To my amazement and relief, I received fair, even favorable treatment at the hands of what I considered to be the aggressive print and electronic media in the large city I was leaving.

What happened in my city? The short version is, I had run out of political capital: said no to too many people, or didn't say yes fast enough to others. But I had carried the mayor's reform banner high with the city council, the organization, and the community.

I had been tackled politically from time to time, but my team had scored frequently. I had probably lost a half step in my running game for a variety of reasons, however.

In previous published writings, I described a force field analysis illustrating what I was up against in making reform changes in a tough-city political environment. But I had been proud of the reform record achieved by "us," not "me."

Another factor contributed to my reduction in political capital. I had been a finalist for the City Manager job in one of the largest cities in the country. After conducting publicized interviews, the city postponed the search for six months. It was a high-profile item in the press and raised questions about my long-term commitment to my city.

Then, weeks on the heels of that fiasco, staff misdirected a long distance phone call intended for my office, instead, to the Mayor's aide. The call was from an Executive Search firm recruiting for a City Manager for another large southwestern city.

I had never initiated any contact with the firm. But, the damage was done. My political capital was low and I was viewed as looking around. No chauvinism intended, but it was like telling your wife you love her and she finds out you've got a date with someone Friday night.

So, what are the lessons we can take away from this experience?

Lesson: Always have an updated résumé and materials ready to go. It's too late to put them together when you need them. The new job I secured was the result of a follow-up résumé that was immediately faxed on the day after the mayor and I talked.

Lesson: Think positively as you carry out your daily duties, but always be ready for the "what if."

Lesson: Conduct yourself with the professionalism and class expected of ICMA members.

Lesson: The harder you work, the luckier you will get.

Lesson: Call ICMA colleagues going through transition. It does make a difference. I remember each call. I was disappointed in some I didn't receive.

Also worth noting, based on the advice of a well-known colleague: (1) this was not pure luck, and (2) there are not always a lot of jobs available when you need them.

I changed jobs in the true manager mode: hard work, years of experience, and strength coming from somewhere when it counted.

Unfortunately, a number of ICMA members in transition don't fare well and go for many months before getting reemployed, as another close colleague has reminded me. There are emotional and family consequences when this happens. It is natural to have feelings of anger and hurt and incur damage to your confidence and self-esteem. I've seen it in the best local government managers in the business.

Lesson: The political process is not always fair or rational. It is the environment we have chosen to work in. Also, our environment is not much different from what private sector, middle management folks go through during mergers and downsizing. A lot of unfairness exists!

Lesson: Pray. I spent time on my knees. It was good for my soul and for my perspective. I was never alone, even when I was by myself.

I love transition stories with happy endings!

REASONS TO BE LET GO

The terrible irony of what I am about to describe is that we know we are in the business of serving elected bodies. We know we serve at their pleasure, not based on our doing a good job or serving the community well, just their whimsical, ever-changing, how-I-feel-today pleasure.

Over the years, I have heard the following reasons given for firing a City Manager:

- The contract is up.
- It's time for a change.
- Since we just had an election, we need our own City Manager.
- He/she's too slow.
- He/she's too fast.
- He/she can't build consensus with the council.
- He/she won't stand up to the unions.
- The unions can't stand him/her.
- He/she's too close to the business community.
- He/she's too high profile, which is the council's job.
- Staff are making too many mistakes, and he/she's in charge of staff.

- A scandal has occurred, someone has to be accountable, and it can't be the council.
- The council wants to go in a different direction (frequently used).
- He/she is not a good City Manager. (This, if true, is a valid reason for a change.)

One reason given to me, by an avowed Republican council member, went like this: "You are a good person and a good manager. We're just used to a Ronald Reagan in the seat, and you're more Al Gore."

The arrow-like words struck even deeper, because they were presented gently, not in anger or spite.

Later, in my anger, I accepted the comparison. Al Gore was intelligent, a good man, a devoted husband and father. I never was a fan of Ronald Reagan.

Nearly every City Manager I have known who exhibited good leadership in tough circumstances or politics has been fired. I believe there is something to be said for long tenure. It is good work if you can get it. It cannot be the final measure of success.

B was City Manager of a small town back in the Midwest. I got to know him when I was a twenty-year-old intern in a nearby city. I marveled at his style, his insight into human psychology, and his quiet dedication to good government practices. What a shame that he was confined to this relative backwater and was an unknown.

Talent can rise to the top, even when the odds are stacked against it. As the years unfolded, he became City Manager of one of the highest profile positions in the country. I was pleased to see a sensitive, talented man succeed and receive the recognition he deserved.

Then, the story I heard: There were stubborn negotiations with the fire union. This was a powerful union, historically difficult.

The mayor and council gave the City Manager his narrow negotiating parameters that he was bound to follow. He followed them with his usual low-key, can-do, we're-all-in-this-together spirit.

A strike ensued.

The strike was messy.

The council expanded the negotiating parameters. The strike was settled. The council fired the City Manager.

Another colleague, D, accepted the City Manager position of a medium-sized community at the young age of twenty-nine. He was exceptionally competent. He introduced modern management, good planning, and the principles of racial integration. He contributed to the profession with a high profile.

D served his community for twenty-three years and then was fired. When I talked to him about it one year after the dismissal, the trauma still resonated. It was in his eyes and his face. He said he went into the evaluation session sure he had three votes. One vote, a long-time friend, voted to fire him.

One remarkable City Manager, L, highly regarded in the profession, moved like clockwork every two years to a new position. He described himself as a change agent. I think he knew something I found out the hard way. I was a change agent too and wanted to move before I got changed.

G was the first City Manager I was introduced to as a young man. He was a star in the profession. Later in his career, he took the reins of one of the largest jurisdictions in the Southern part of the country.

There was a problem in the assessments that went out to the property owners. The responsibility for that lay with a separately elected official and was not part of the City Manager's portfolio. The City Manager was fired.

A former intern of mine, who was working for him at the time, noted that G's performance evaluation, before they fired him, was in public and four hours long. He went toe-to-toe, without a single break. I think I was most impressed that he had done it without a bathroom break.

It seems like a perilous journey. But, it is exciting. Beats making widgets for a living.

Lesson: Be sure you take your bathroom break before you go into an evaluation session with elected officials.

ON MY WATCH

I pulled into the dark, rain-soaked parking lot on a wintry Friday night, at six o'clock. I was headed for a neighborhood meeting in the all-Black neighborhood. It had been another difficult week wrestling with no-win issues at city hall.

The very long council meeting that week spewed acrimony. The elected officials didn't know how to play together in the same sandbox and share their toys. They had elevated throwing sand into the gears of government to an art level.

I wanted to go home, have a beer, and hang with my kids.

I stepped out of my car and proceeded up the sidewalk. I noticed a youngish, nice-looking Black couple with their twelve-year-old son moving in the same direction. An unusually handsome boy with a dazzling smile, he was confined to a wheelchair.

I recognized the family immediately from the old news reports. Their son had been shot in a drive-by one year before in a crime that was random, senseless.

I didn't say anything, but as we were walking, the mother said to me, "Excuse me, aren't you our City Manager?"

I said yes, I was, and smiled hesitantly.

She turned to her son and said, "Look, it's our City Manager, and he's visiting our neighborhood tonight. Isn't that wonderful!"

There was no sarcasm, no bitterness, just genuine friendliness.

I was speechless. I was the City Manager of this city, her young son had been shot and permanently paralyzed on my watch, and she was thanking me for coming to visit her neighborhood!

I introduced myself.

She said, "Thank you for coming."

All I could say was, "You are welcome."

You can't imagine how I felt then and how I still feel to this day.

Like I said, it was on my watch.

Lesson: When you are City Manager, everything is on your watch.

DEAR JOHN

Dear John,

It's been over a year. I wanted to extend to you and Jane a warm holiday greeting.

I must thank you again for renting me the room in your home in that fantastic neighborhood. It presented some of the most dramatic topography I have ever seen. You provided me with a home away from home, while I worked for the city.

I greatly enjoyed our association. As I told you before, I took an instant liking to you when I first met you. I think it was the combination of your having studied Latin, like me; your wry, dry sense of humor; and your kindness.

Not many folks can speak Latin like we could.

As I got to know you better, I was impressed with your having been in the Catholic seminary, being offered a contract to pitch for the New York Yankees, and serving as a high-ranking member of the Ford and Nixon administrations.

All the movie stars you hung out with years ago to raise money for the child development foundation left an impression on me also; especially since you were interested in only what they could do for the foundation, and not a bit bedazzled by their fame.

I respected the fact that you beat cancer twice, although I could see the faraway look in your eyes that told me the toll it had taken.

The killer credential, though, was your good judgment in marrying Jane years ago and raising three remarkable children, all now successful, caring adults.

The room in your house provided a safe refuge. I was very tired of the weekly eight-hundred-mile roundtrip job commute, more than I wanted to recognize. I will tell you it really made me appreciate my time at home with my family.

Thanks for listening to my job woes. I tried to keep the complaints brief, but sometimes I just had to vent, or I would have bust. I gave the job 100 percent and felt good about the record of accomplishment. But, I was very frustrated with the horrible organizational ethos and scattered, disorganized third-rate physical facilities.

Since I stayed with you guys, I've started to accept my retirement, even though I still had plenty of juice at the time and wanted to stay engaged. I've taken up writing. I'm focusing on the three R's: reading, 'riting, and running.

I haven't talked to Jane in months. The last time we chatted on the phone, she thanked me again for helping her when you had your stroke. I still vividly remember her coming into my room at 6:00

AM, asking if I could help because you were on the floor and couldn't move.

My contribution was to cover you up and direct Jane to call 911 immediately, which she did. Minimal contribution on my part, but I always glowed in her appreciation for my minor assistance. I think it was important just to be there, too.

I was impressed with the daily progress that you made in your rehabilitation at the hospital. I know it was tough for you to be so reliant on others.

I'm sorry I had to leave before you could fully recover. Two weeks after we said our good-byes and I moved back home, I was in the area for a job interview and stopped in at the hospital. They told me you weren't a patient there anymore and they couldn't give me any more information. When I pressed, they looked at me funny and said I needed to call the family.

I called Jane and then your daughter, leaving messages.

Your daughter called me on my cell phone that evening. She told me you had died the previous day.

I have to tell you once again how very much I just enjoyed knowing you and Jane. You made me realize that angels are real, the human kind. I believe we are all called to be angels to one another. I can't thank you enough.

You still reside in my heart. I'll see you on the other side.

Some Real Leadership

Political leadership takes many forms. The most effective leadership communicates that we're a team, all in this together. It looks like this from an elected official: "I know it's 1:15 AM, but let's continue our discussion until we're done" leadership.

The key ingredients for long-term success seem to be the low-key, give-everyone-else-credit, fantastic-listening-skills type of leadership.

There were two high-profile mayors who took center stage as I played a supporting role.

In one, as an executive intern, I witnessed the first Black mayor of a major American city take over the reins. With his positive, engaging charm, he sought to breathe life into a city headed for life support. It was also a city where controversial shootings took place with Black militants and police exchanging gunfire, with later cover-ups by the police.

Later, in my role as City Manager, I worked for an exceptionally high-profile mayor of a large city. Now, you might expect, as I did, that he was engaged in an all-show, what's-in-it-for-me political career.

It was not like that, at all.

It took a while to sink in, but he really meant it when he put me in charge of reforming city hall. He wanted me to challenge the municipal organization away from "good enough" and propel it toward excellence.

While I wrestled alligators at city hall, he strengthened relationships with the state capitol and the Office of the President of the United States. He was a compelling advocate for the community.

Word came back that the president, impressed with the new reform energy our mayor was leading with, told his federal cabinet: "See what you can do for this mayor. He's moving his city in the right direction."

The mayor also took on the local educational establishment, calling for a new day: one in which the children, our future, would actually receive an education. Forget the finger pointing and just overhaul the system was his position.

He took on everyone, regardless of political blowback, if the future of his city required it: former supporters, business moguls, developers, unions, city councilmen, the press, and even his good friend the governor.

I was in City Manager heaven.

Here's the most powerful snapshot that succinctly captures this leadership and mindset:

I had just been publicly introduced as the new City Manager. After the press conference, the mayor invited me to lunch. We chatted for a while before ordering our food.

In chitchat, casual conversation, two guys BS-ing, the mayor started describing the interrelationships among poverty, education, personal expectations, land use, crime, employment, prison recidivism, and on and on.

I sat there thinking, "Wait a minute! I'm the one with two master's degrees and thirty years' municipal experience and all the awards! Yet, this TV-star guy is informally delivering a brilliant, nuanced, mini-lecture on the nature of urban affairs."

I immediately looked at him in a different light, realizing that the good ole boy accent camouflaged an insightful, analytical mind.

But then, the icing on the cake, or maybe the cake itself: The waiters brought the food. I was prattling on, trying to keep up with the mayor. Suddenly, there was a silence. The mayor was looking down at his lap. Had I said something to offend him?

No, he was praying before eating. Shame on me that it took me more than a nanosecond to recognize it. And, why wasn't I doing the same? I was brought up to do that. What happened? This was a pretty interesting fellow.

The duty in that city was politically tough. It was dog years, with each year the equivalent of three years someplace else.

I needed to regularly plug into the mayor's optimistic, take-the-hill, high energy. Up to that point, I had spent most of my career running on my own gas fumes in each city.

This scene was different and exhilarating. But, if I didn't have his cheerleading advice every three days or so, I fell into a funk.

I think and speak fondly of him to this day.

THE "THIN GRAY LINE" OF CITY MANAGERS READY TO SERVE LOCAL GOVERNMENT

RULE #1: DO NOT FALL ON YOUR OWN SWORD.

THE THIN GRAY LINE

I am a gray man, one who defines himself by being part of a larger institution, enjoying the structure, the norms, and the established definitions of success or failure.

I gradually realized that in city management, whether you are a gray man (or woman), you become part of "the thin gray line."

We all know what the thin blue line is: the guys and gals in the blue uniforms, cops, who protect our streets. The thin gray line protects the cops and more.

The thin gray line sprang from the roots of the reform movement in the early 1900s to combat rampant corruption in local government throughout the country.

The thin gray line advances the cause of good government in the face of corruption, status quo, and political foolishness. Quite a recipe for action. We should never move away from these roots. It's not about business as usual.

Sometimes my self-talk, my internal self-criticism, has taken a left turn and beat me up for not having a more winsome personality, being more diplomatic, or being more touchy-feely. But, as Popeye the Sailor Man said, "I'm am what I'm am."

I have wondered why I have an edge, and I believe it's because of my impatience. I want my organizations to run faster, better, and cheaper. In my case, it's a combination of personality and mission and a desire to make a difference. It borders on messianism.

I unrealistically expect all elected officials to do the right thing for their communities. After all, they were raised there and have friends, families, and businesses. I'm just the hired help, as some have reminded me along the way.

God Bless you in the thin gray line!

It's All About
The People

I'm a type A personality: high energy, driven, outcome oriented.

Years ago, I aspired to be more of a type B personality: relaxed, calm, people oriented. I gave up on that personality transformation in recognition that I am who I am and could just as easily have a heart attack in mode B, out of boredom, as in mode A.

Besides, A is more interesting with its fast pace.

What impressed me though is having read the reflections of another City Manager with the same temperament. As he looked back at the end of his career, he commented that it was really all about the people.

He couldn't remember all the successful projects, certainly didn't want to remember all the meetings, but he did remember all the people, especially the good people: the good mayors, the good council members, the great staff, and the community folks.

For me, I think it was especially about the great staff, people who had shared a common vision, served in the trenches together, and at the end of the day had run the race and fought the fight for good government.

I Did It My Way

Finally, one day it hit me. I saw what this City Manager was doing. He followed a real simple ethic with friendly integrity and openness, treating people with respect and holding employees accountable while providing strong support for them, against all odds.

I thought, "I like how he does his city management."

In fact, if that's the way you were supposed to do it, I thought I now had enough tools in the toolbox to do it.

Besides, I had concluded from direct experience that there is no complete job protection anywhere, anyhow. If they want to get you, they will. I figured I might as well have a contract as a City Manager. At least I would have a little more control over my life.

Oh, yeah, there were now two more darling little mouths to feed, and each month I was dipping into my savings. I needed to make more money.

So, I embarked on the shark-infested, alligator-swimming, piranha-filled waters of city management.

But, I told myself, we'd have to do it the right way to increase the chances of success. If I risked being shot out of the saddle, then it would be because I was sitting tall in the saddle.

This became an apt analogy, because we did have *High Noon* moments, with Gary Cooper sweating it out alone, except for his faithful wife.

Unfortunately, I didn't look like Gary, and life didn't always end like the movie…Wait a minute, it did! Gary left town with his wife at the end of the movie, and so did I!

Here's how I thought it needed to be done. If we had these understandings in place, we'd be holding the banner of city management high:

A PHILOSOPHY OF GOVERNANCE. The role of city hall is more than repairing the streets and picking up the garbage. Those things are important and must be done right, but city hall should also be thinking about the health, safety, and future of the entire community, not just maintaining.

My job needs to be more than playing desk jockey and shuffling papers. I can shuffle paper with the best of them. I need to encourage the city staff, the mayor, council, and the citizenry to step up to meet the challenges of asking: "Who are we as a community?" "Where do we want to go?" "How will we get there?"

We should not be afraid of vigorous debate on these questions, and we should come together after the debate. An united community can work miracles.

MAXIMIZE THE ROLE OF THE ELECTED OFFICIAL. Today, in government, there are so many appointed boards and commissions and professional staff responsibilities that have influence over community life. Those are helpful roles. But, we need to remind ourselves that in the representative democracy we have, the only true legitimacy lies with the elected official.

That's why I continually remind myself that the only elective office I've ever held was as junior class vice president in college, and I wasn't a very good one.

COMMITMENT TO GOOD GOVERNMENT. Good government is open government. If Jane or Joe Taxpayer walks in the door of city hall and asks why we are spending money a certain way, or any other question, we need to explain the issue in such a way that a reasonable person would be satisfied.

The preamble to the State of Texas Public Information Act captures this point well, in a paraphrase:

The American constitutional form of representative government holds to the principle that government is the servant of the people and not the master of them...The people, in delegating authority, do not give their public servants the right to decide what is good for the people to know and what is not good for them to know. The people insist on remaining informed so that they may retain control over the instruments they have created.

RESPECT FOR PUBLIC SERVICE — A TRUST. The work that City Managers do in local government is some of the most important work going on in the country. It is building community in this huge country/continent and in a culture that is hungry for a sense of place.

City Managers serve a community of people who rely on their local government for important services.

POSITIVE RELATIONSHIP WITH ELECTED OFFICIALS. I have always striven to create and foster a relationship characterized by ensuring trust, sharing maximum information, conducting an open administration, establishing mutual respect, playing no favorites on the elected body, and minimizing surprises.

Boy, do elected officials hate surprises! Well, we all do.

Yes, I truly wanted those platitudinous words to be the hallmark of our relationship. Was it?

If it had been, I wouldn't have moved around so much, would I? So, what happened?

What happened were all the things you've been reading about here, a gray man with messianic tendencies who is a sheepdog.

I played it straight. But, I also took on some tough political assignments.

COLLABORATIVE MANAGEMENT STYLE. In the job interviews, we're always asked about our management style. I like the answer I developed over the years.

I say that if someone who reports to me is hardworking and dedicated to the work we're doing in the public sector, then that person will find me interesting, challenging, and fun to work for. I have high expectations of staff on purpose.

However, sometimes you are dealing with a person who has retired on the job. I've seen that happen at age twenty-five and thirty-five, as well as older years. If that's the case, then the employee will find me an overly demanding, difficult supervisor.

I want city staff to be excited about their work. I recognize my responsibility for setting the stage for that. I want them charged up so I can turn them loose to work with the community.

I follow these five steps:

1. Select good people.
2. Be clear on goals or directions.
3. Step back and let them do their jobs.
4. Monitor performance.
5. Correct and reward performance.

I believe in tapping every resource we have as an organization. I will cross departmental and personnel boundaries easily.

For example, if the police chief has something to contribute on a planning or transportation issue, then the chief needs to be brought into that discussion. Likewise, if a law enforcement problem can get help from the people in the recreation department, then we need to include them.

ABILITY TO MAKE TOUGH DECISIONS. I'm like everyone else. I want to be well thought of. However, the job doesn't always let you be everybody's best friend. On the tough, day-to-day issues, the buck stops at my desk.

ABILITY TO DELIVER BAD NEWS. We've all heard, "Don't shoot the messenger." Saying this doesn't do any good. People naturally react to he who is saying what we don't want to hear.

The City Manager and the staff must present the facts and the alternatives, along with a recommendation to the elected body. We are not doing our jobs if we merely tell them what we think they want to hear. If we do that, we should be fired.

If the elected officials do not like what they are hearing and want to bash someone, the only person they are allowed to bash is me. I serve at their pleasure. How often have I seen the light of pleasure dim in their eyes as the professional, full-of-integrity City Manager presents the facts of the situation in question.

PROTECT THE CITY'S FINANCIAL POSTURE. This is a critical component, because without healthy finances, we cannot do all of the good things we need to do in providing services and improving the community.

We must stay invested in the community's physical infrastructure, from street lights to water systems. We've been hearing for decades how we have not done that across the nation. Bridges are starting to collapse.

We must have a healthy and diverse tax base, utilizing the economic development strategies that apply to our respective communities. Not all communities have the same vision for themselves, and that's fine.

We should be conservative on expenditures, treating each tax dollar as if it were our own. There's not supposed to be a Democratic or Republican way to sweep the streets or pick up the garbage.

We are obliged to stretch that hard-earned tax dollar by every means possible. We should keep the door open for options, always trying to figure out how our government can run faster, better, and cheaper.

Does privatization of a service offer savings? Do we need to reexamine our user fees or charges? Someone is paying. Who is paying? And, what is fair?

We should use as few employees as possible by utilizing core staffing, cross-training, and contract and part-time personnel. Full-time, classified employees are very expensive.

I have always promoted attracting the best talent available and paying that talent well for good performance. I then prefer to supplement that talent with part-time or contract personnel as needed to deal with special projects or peak work loads.

There's another reason for paying people fairly and well.

People are the most important investment we can make. It's not the police cars that patrol and protect the community. It's not the fire trucks that put out fires.

Many times the people who do these things for us are our friends, relatives, and neighbors. They are not anonymous bureaucrats. *They are us.*

CLOSING

Let's use my daughter's question to me years ago, when she was just nine: "Daddy, do you like your job?"

Answer: "Mostly yes, sometimes no."

What I like: City management is meaningful, important work, making an impact on a community of people. There is enormous opportunity to make things happen.

What I don't like: There is never enough time to do all the things that you feel need to be done. And it is hard to be a target of criticism, even when you are doing the right thing.

Yes, it has been a great ride. When I married my wife, a young bride, I promised to show her the country. She was excited. I hadn't planned on showing her the country through a number of City Manager assignments.

My favorite quote is an excerpt from the citizenship oath of ancient Athens. It spells out our duty and responsibility in this business of city management, and it acknowledges that we must fight the good fight, whether we succeed or fail:

> *We will strive to quicken the public's sense of civic duty; and thus in all the ways we will strive to transmit this city not less but greater, better and more beautiful than it was transmitted to us.*

Appendix: Job Interviews

The following is a list of jurisdictions where I was interviewed during the course of my career.

At midpoint in my career, I concluded I needed to hustle, be fast on my feet, and stay ahead of the political ax. I tended to develop options when I could.

Correct that; I needed to develop options all the time.

Arlington County, Virginia
Beaumont, Texas
Bellevue, Washington
Beverly Hills, California
Bloomington, Minnesota
Boulder, Colorado
Brea, California
Broward County, Florida
Carson, California
Charles County, Maryland
Clearlake, California
Cleveland, Ohio
Coachella, California
Coalinga, California
Collinsville, Illinois

Colton, California
Columbia, Maryland
Corpus Christi, Texas
Cupertino, California
Dallas, Texas
Dallas County, Texas
Dayton, Ohio
Englewood, Colorado
Eugene, Oregon
Farmington Hills, Michigan
Fort Lauderdale, Florida
Fresno, California
Greenbelt, Maryland
Greenwood Village, Colorado
Greeley, Colorado
Hanford, California
Hayward, California
Indio, California
Irvine, California
Killeen, Texas
Leesburg, Virginia
Lincoln, California
Livermore, California
Marin County, California
Monterey County, California
Montgomery County, Maryland
Narragansett, Rhode Island
Orange County, California
Pensacola, Florida
Pleasanton, California
Pomona, California
Prince George's County, Maryland
Pueblo, Colorado

Redding, California
Redlands, California
Reedley, California
Rialto, California
Richmond, California
Rockville, Maryland
Sacramento, California
San Antonio, Texas
San Bernardino, California
San Diego Utility District, California
San Fernando, California
Santa Clara County, California
Stanislaus County, California
Stockton, California
Tempe, Arizona
Tracy, California
Tulare, California
US Department of Housing and Urban Development
Upland, California
Washington, DC
West Covina, California
Wyoming, Michigan
Yorba Linda, California

MAYBE YOU COULD SAY I WAS ALWAYS ON THE RUN.

Made in the USA
Middletown, DE
23 February 2020